Islam, Marxism, and Social Change

Historical Materialism Book Series

VOLUME 403

The titles published in this series are listed at *brill.com/hm*

Islam, Marxism, and Social Change

Emile Tuma's *Social Movements in Islam*

Edited and annotated by

Abed Kanaaneh

Translated by

Ruba Simaan

BRILL

ISSN 1570-1522
ISBN 978-90-04-77425-4
ISBN 978-90-04-77426-1 (PDF)
DOI https://doi.org/10.1163/9789004774261

Library of Congress Control Number: 2026948619

Brill and Koninklijke Brill BV are part of De Gruyter Brill.
www.degruyterbrill.com

Questions about General Product Safety Regulation: productsafety@degruyterbrill.com

Contents

PART 1

Revolutionary Heritage: Emile Tuma and Reclaiming Progressive Traditions in Islam

Abed Kanaaneh

CHAPTER 1

The Making of a Revolutionary Intellectual: Short Biography of Emile Tuma

1 Early Life, Education and Early Activism

Emile Tuma was born on 16 March 1919 in Haifa to a Christian Palestinian family during the final years of Ottoman rule in Palestine. His upbringing in Haifa, a major port city with significant diversity and political ferment, exposed him early on to the complex dynamics of colonial rule, ethnic relations, and emerging nationalist movements.

Tuma received his primary education at the Orthodox Community School in Haifa, an institution that served the Palestinian community. His secondary education was completed in 1937 at the Bishop English Missionary School in Jerusalem, also known as Zion College. This educational trajectory, spanning both Haifa and Jerusalem, exposed him to British colonial educational systems while also connecting him to broader networks of Palestinian intellectual and political activity.

During his high school years at Zion College, Tuma became increasingly drawn to nationalist and leftist student activities. Two figures proved particularly influential in shaping his political consciousness. His Arabic language teacher, the progressive writer Raif Khoury (1913–67), introduced him to ideas of revolutionary justice and anti-colonial struggle. Additionally, his colleague Abdullah Bandak (1910–74), a communist journalist, helped orient Tuma toward Marxist analysis and international socialism. These intellectual influences would prove foundational to his later development as both political activist and historian.[1]

Upon completing secondary school in 1937, Tuma gained admission to study law at Cambridge University in Britain. This opportunity represented significant social mobility for a Palestinian from Haifa, reflecting both his academic abilities and his family's resources. However, the outbreak of World War II in September 1939 prevented him from traveling to Britain to begin his studies, fundamentally altering his life trajectory.

1 Al-Sharif 1991.

 | HTTPS://DOI.ORG/10.1163/9789004774261-002

The disruption of his university plans coincided with Tuma's deepening political engagement. In late 1939, he joined the clandestine Palestinian Communist Party, marking the beginning of his lifelong commitment to revolutionary politics. The Palestinian Communist Party operated under severe restrictions during the British Mandate, requiring members to maintain strict secrecy while organising among both Arab and Jewish workers.

Tuma's early political work focused on organising students and intellectuals, drawing on his educational background and connections within Palestinian urban society. Together with Tawfiq Toubi (1922–2011), who would become a prominent communist leader, Tuma founded the 'Ray of Hope Club' (*nadi shuʿaʿ al-amal*) in mid-1942. This organisation served as a front for communist organising among educated Palestinians while providing cultural and political programming that challenged both British colonial authority and emerging Zionist institutions.[2]

As World War II intensified, the wartime economy created new opportunities for labor organising. Tuma became deeply involved in the revitalised union movement, working to organise Arab workers who were increasingly employed in war-related industries. His efforts culminated in November 1942 when he helped establish the Federation of Arab Trade Unions and Associations, which grew to include tens of thousands of Arab workers across Palestine. This represented one of the most significant organisational achievements of the Palestinian labor movement during the Mandate period.[3]

Building on this success, Tuma and several comrades – including Tawfiq Toubi, Emile Habibi (1922–96), and Boulos Farah (1910–91) – established the National Liberation League (*'Usbat al-Taharur al-Wattani*) in September 1943.[4] Tuma was elected Secretary-General of this organisation, which represented an attempt to create a broader anti-colonial front that could unite Palestinian nationalist struggle with international communist solidarity. The National Liberation League advocated for Palestinian independence while maintaining internationalist perspectives that distinguished it from other nationalist organisations.[5]

On 14 May 1944, the Federation of Arab Workers' Unions and Associations launched *al-Ittihad* (Unity), a weekly newspaper that served as the primary voice for Arab workers in Palestine. Tuma became the official owner and re-

2 Amal 1989.

3 *Al-Ittihad* 2019.

4 For the founding of the National Liberation League, see Budeiri 1979, pp. 139–65.

5 *Al-Ittihad* 2019. On the ideological tensions within Palestinian nationalism during this period, see Sayigh 1997, pp. 35–57.

sponsible editor, establishing a platform that would remain central to Palestinian communist politics for decades. Under his editorship, *al-Ittihad* developed a distinctive approach that combined class-based analysis with Palestinian nationalist themes, challenging both British colonial policies and Zionist settlement while advocating for Arab-Jewish working-class solidarity.

2 The Nakba and Adapting to Israeli Rule

The events of 1948 brought profound upheaval to Tuma's life and to Palestinian society generally. While carrying out partisan directives in Lebanon in April 1948, Tuma was detained by Lebanese authorities and held in the Baalbek detention center. His imprisonment occurred during the most critical period of the 1948 Arab-Israeli War, when Palestinian society was experiencing systematic destruction and mass displacement.

Tuma's incarceration lasted until October 1948, during which time he was held alongside Palestinian and Lebanese communist detainees. He later wrote about this experience in *Al-Jadid*,[6] providing insights into both the personal trauma of imprisonment and the broader political dynamics affecting communist movements during this period. His detention prevented him from participating directly in the events that would transform Palestine into Israel and create the Palestinian refugee crisis.[7]

Upon his release in October 1948 and subsequent return to Haifa, Tuma found himself in dramatically changed circumstances. The Palestinian society he had known was largely destroyed, with approximately 750,000 Palestinians displaced from their homes. The approximately 150,000 Palestinians who remained within the new state of Israel, including Tuma himself, found themselves transformed overnight from a majority population in Mandatory Palestine to a marginalised minority under Israeli rule.

Tuma's return to Haifa in 1949 marked the beginning of a new phase in his political and intellectual career. He resumed his activism within what became the Communist Party of Israel, using platforms like *al-Ittihad* and the cultural journal *al-Jadid* (founded in 1951) to articulate a vision of national liberation and social justice adapted to the new realities of Israeli state control.

---

6 Tuma wrote about this experience in the Lebanese detention centre alongside Palestinian and Lebanese communist detainees in an article published in *Al-Jadid*, 7, 2, May 1955, pp. 39–46.

7 On the destruction of Palestinian society during 1948, see Pappe 2006.

The Communist Party of Israel faced unique challenges as it attempted to maintain both Arab and Jewish membership while operating within a state defined by Zionist ideology.[8] Tuma played crucial roles in developing theoretical frameworks that could address Palestinian national aspirations while maintaining internationalist communist principles. His editorship of *al-Ittihad* proved particularly important in this regard, as the newspaper became the primary voice for Palestinian political consciousness within Israel.

During the 1950s and early 1960s, Tuma began developing the historical and theoretical approaches that would define his mature intellectual work. He and his colleagues contributed regularly to *Al-Jadid*, exploring Islamic history and heritage through Marxist analytical frameworks. Articles on the Qarmatians, the Zanj Revolution, and other Islamic social movements laid the groundwork for his later comprehensive treatment in *Social Movements in Islam*.

His engagement with Islamic intellectual history during this period was not merely academic but responded to practical political challenges facing Palestinian communists. As Islamic movements began gaining influence in the broader Arab world, Palestinian communist intellectuals needed frameworks for engaging with religious tradition that neither dismissed it as false consciousness nor accepted it uncritically. Tuma's historical work provided analytical tools for this engagement.

3 Intellectual Maturation and Major Works

In mid-1965, Tuma was invited to join the Orientalist Institute in Moscow, marking a significant phase in his intellectual development. This opportunity provided him access to Soviet academic resources and methodologies while connecting him to broader networks of Marxist scholars studying the Middle East and Islamic history.

During his time in Moscow, Tuma encountered Hussein Muruwwa (1909–87), a prominent communist leader of the Lebanese Communist Party and author of *al-Naz'at al-Madiyya fi al-Falsafa al-'Arabiyya al-Islamiyya* (Materialist Tendencies in Arab-Islamic Philosophy). The friendship that developed between these two intellectuals proved mutually influential, as both were grappling with similar theoretical challenges regarding the application of historical materialism to Islamic intellectual history. Their collaboration and intellectual exchange helped refine approaches to analyzing Islamic heritage through Marxist frameworks that would characterise both scholars' mature work.

8 Beinin 1990.

Tuma's academic focus during this period centered on the history of the contemporary Middle East, building upon his earlier political experience and historical interests. His comprehensive research culminated in receiving a doctorate in history from the Soviet Academy of Sciences in recognition of his work *The Journey of the Arab Peoples and the Problems of Arab Unity*. This academic achievement represented formal recognition of his scholarly contributions while providing him with additional theoretical tools for his subsequent historical analyses.

The 1967 Arab-Israeli War marked another turning point in Tuma's career. Israel's occupation of the West Bank and Gaza Strip reconnected Palestinians within Israel with their counterparts in the occupied territories, creating new possibilities for political organising while also introducing new challenges as Islamic movements began gaining influence among Palestinians in Israel.

During this period, Tuma produced his most significant historical works. *The Roots of the Palestinian Question* (1968) offered a Marxist interpretation of Palestinian history that emphasised the interconnectedness of national and class struggles. *The History of the Modern March of the Arab Peoples* (1979) extended this analysis to the broader Arab world, providing frameworks for understanding how colonial domination and class formation shaped modern Arab societies.

His masterwork, *Social Movements in Islam* (1979), represented the culmination of decades of engagement with Islamic intellectual history. This book analyzed major Islamic social and intellectual movements – including the Muʿtazila, Shuʿubiyya, Qarmatians, and others – through historical materialist frameworks, demonstrating how theological developments reflected underlying social contradictions and class struggles.

The book appeared at a crucial moment, just as the 1979 Iranian Revolution was reshaping politics throughout the Islamic world. Tuma's analysis provided Palestinian and Arab leftists with intellectual resources for engaging with the rising tide of political Islam, showing how Islamic tradition contained both progressive and reactionary elements that could be distinguished through materialist analysis.

Throughout the 1970s and early 1980s, Tuma remained active in Palestinian political organising within Israel. He was instrumental in forming the Democratic Front for Peace and Equality (Hadash) in 1977, which brought together the Communist Party of Israel with other progressive forces to create a broader electoral alliance. This represented an attempt to move beyond the communist party's traditional base among Palestinian workers to appeal to broader segments of Palestinian society within Israel.

Tuma also chaired the Preparatory Committee for the 1980 'Conference of the Arab Masses with the Participation of the Jewish Democratic Forces', an ambitious attempt to unite progressive forces across ethnic and national lines. These initiatives reflected his belief that successful resistance to Israeli policies required building coalitions that could challenge the state's divide-and-rule strategies.[9]

His role as an organic intellectual – in Gramscian terms – proved particularly important during this period. Tuma understood that Palestinian political movements needed not only organisational structures but also intellectual frameworks that could help Palestinians maintain their identity and aspirations while operating within the constraints of Israeli citizenship. His historical work provided resources for this cultural and intellectual resistance.

4 Legacy and Death (1985)

Emile Tuma died in 1985, leaving behind a substantial body of historical scholarship and a legacy of political organising that significantly shaped Palestinian political consciousness within Israel. His funeral, covered extensively in *Al-Ittihad*, was attended by thousands of Palestinians who recognised his contributions to both intellectual and political life.

As a researcher and historian, Tuma authored fifteen books and hundreds of articles published between 1962 and his death. His bibliography demonstrates the breadth of his intellectual engagement:

> *The Arabs and Historical Development in the Middle East* (1962); *The July 23 Revolution in its First Decade* (1962); *The Roots of the Palestinian Question* (1968); *American Policy in the Middle East* (1973); *30 Years of Al-Ittihad – People's Diaries* (1974); *Sixty Years of the Palestinian Arab National Movement* (1978); *Social Movements in Islam* (1979); *The History of the Modern March of the Arab Peoples* (1979); *Revolutionary Process in Islam* (1981); *The Path of the Arab Masses' Struggle in Israel* (1982); *Contemporary Zionism* (1982); *Palestine in the Ottoman Era* (1983); *The Arab National Movement and the Palestinian Question* (1984); *The Palestine Liberation Organisation* (1986); and *Selections from Literary Criticism* (1993).[10]

9 Al-Ittihad 1985.
10 Amal 1989.

Within Palestinian society, Tuma's legacy includes both his specific historical analyses and his broader approach to engaging with cultural tradition. His insistence that Palestinian leftists needed to understand and engage with Islamic heritage rather than dismissing it provided frameworks that remain relevant for contemporary progressive movements in Islamic societies.

The limited circulation of his work beyond Palestinian communist circles – due to political barriers, the marginalisation of communist movements, and the complexity of his theoretical approach – means that his contributions remain relatively unknown compared to other Arab intellectuals of his generation. However, recent scholarly interest in non-Eurocentric approaches to Marxist theory and Islamic studies has led to renewed engagement with his methodological innovations.

Tuma's life trajectory – from a middle-class Christian Palestinian student destined for Cambridge to a communist intellectual operating within Israel – reflects the broader transformations that shaped twentieth-century Palestinian society. His ability to maintain both Palestinian nationalist commitments and internationalist socialist principles while operating within an Israeli state defined by Zionist ideology represents a unique form of intellectual and political resistance that continues to offer insights for contemporary struggles over identity, tradition, and political transformation.

CHAPTER 2

Social Movements in Islam: A Marxist Reading of the History of Islam

The 1970s marked a decisive moment in Marxist theoretical engagement with religious movements, particularly in relation to Islamic history. This period witnessed a profound transformation in how historical materialist analysis approached religious phenomena, moving beyond earlier reductionist frameworks to develop more sophisticated theoretical tools. Two major developments shaped this intellectual landscape, producing new ways of understanding the relationship between religious movements and class consciousness.

The first significant shift came with the crisis of orthodox Marxism and its traditional treatment of religion as a mere ideological superstructure. Influenced by Gramsci's analysis of popular consciousness and Althusser's theory of ideological state apparatuses,[1] scholars began developing more nuanced approaches to religious movements. These new theoretical frameworks recognised how religious movements could articulate class interests while maintaining relative autonomy from economic determination. This theoretical innovation proved particularly fruitful for understanding Islamic social movements.

Simultaneously, the 1960s and 1970s saw the emergence of distinctive Arab Marxist theoretical traditions. Scholars like Hussein Muruwwa, Tayyib Tizini and Emile Tuma worked to develop theoretical frameworks that could account for the specificity of Islamic societies while maintaining historical materialist analysis.[2] Their work represented a significant challenge to both orthodox Marxist reductionism and orientalist essentialism, creating new possibilities for understanding the relationship between religious consciousness and social transformation.

To understand the distinctiveness of Tuma's theoretical contribution, it is essential to situate his work within the broader landscape of Marxist approaches to Islamic history that had emerged since the early twentieth century. Tuma's analysis built upon, but significantly diverged from, established Soviet approaches to Islamic societies that had been developing since the 1920s.

1 Gramsci 1971; Althusser 1971.
2 Muruwwa 1988; Tizzini 1978.

 | HTTPS://DOI.ORG/10.1163/9789004774261-003

Early Soviet scholars like Evgeny Beliaev and Vasily Bartold had applied historical materialism to Islamic societies, focusing primarily on economic structures and class formation. The Soviet Academy's multi-volume History of the Peoples of the East (1956) established comprehensive frameworks for analysing pre-capitalist Islamic societies through stages of historical development, emphasising the transition from tribal formations through feudalism toward capitalism. However, these Soviet approaches often suffered from mechanical determinism – treating religious phenomena as simple reflections of economic base without accounting for their relative autonomy or dialectical complexity. Soviet scholars typically categorised Islamic movements as either 'progressive' (supporting social transformation) or 'reactionary' (defending existing order), without examining how movements could transform dialectically from one character to another as material conditions changed.

Tuma's work also engaged with more sophisticated Marxist analysis of Islamic societies, particularly Maxime Rodinson's ground-breaking *Islam and Capitalism*, which predated Tuma's *al-Harakat* by more than a decade. Rodinson's work provided crucial theoretical groundwork by demonstrating that Islamic doctrine contained no inherent barriers to capitalist development – contrary to both Orientalist claims about Islamic 'economic backwardness' and romantic Islamic assertions about incompatibility with materialism.[3] Rodinson showed that religious interpretation was historically contingent, with the same Quranic verses justifying different economic practices depending on social context, thus requiring modification of Weber's Protestant Ethic thesis when applied to Islamic societies.

While Tuma clearly benefited from Rodinson's theoretical innovations, his approach diverged in significant ways. Where Rodinson focused on compatibility between Islamic doctrine and capitalist relations, Tuma investigated how Islamic movements articulated class struggle within pre-capitalist formations. Rodinson asked whether Islam permitted capitalism; Tuma asked how Islamic movements expressed social contradictions in their historical contexts. This represented a shift from doctrinal analysis – examining Islamic texts for economic implications – to movement analysis – examining how different social groups used Islamic discourse to articulate their material interests and political aspirations.

The most proximate scholarly antecedent to Emile Tuma's seminal work *al-Harakat* can be found in the pioneering contribution of the Palestinian-Russian intellectual Bandali al-Jawzi (1871–1942). In 1928, al-Jawzi published *min Tarikh*

3 Rodinson 1981 [1973].

al-Harkat al-Fikriyya fi al-Islam (History of Islamic Intellectual Movements),[4] which represents the first documented attempt in Arab scholarly discourse to examine Islamic historiography through a Marxist analytical framework.[5] While al-Jawzi's theoretical intervention laid important groundwork, his analysis was more limited in scope compared to Tuma's later comprehensive treatment. Moreover, the distinct socio-political contexts within which these works emerged – al-Jawzi writing under the British Mandate in Palestine during the late 1920s, and Tuma producing his scholarship as part of the Palestinian Arab minority in Israel in the 1970s – necessarily influenced their respective analytical approaches and conclusions.[6]

In his book, al-Jawzi focused on movements close to socialism in Islamic history, such as the Babic revolution, the Ismaʿili movement, and the Qarmatians. Emile Tuma went further, dealing with movements and intellectual tendencies that were far from socialism but had a significant impact on the development of thought within Islamic civilisation, such as Shiites in general, Muʿtazilites, Ashʿari, shoʿubiyya, and other movements that had nothing to do directly with socialist ideas. Still, he analysed their social and class roots to highlight their contribution to the development (or regression) of Islamic and Arab societies.

Tuma (like Muruwwa and Tizini) also challenged other Arab Marxist thinkers such as Jurj Tarabishi and Sadiq Jalal al-ʿAzm who adopted a revolutionary stance that called for a complete break with *turath*.[7] Al-ʿAzm criticised the tendency to use *turath* as a refuge from contemporary challenges.[8]

Tuma's and Muruwwa's approach to *turath* was groundbreaking in its application of historical materialism to Arab-Islamic philosophical heritage. In his seminal work *Al-Nazʿat al-Madiyya fil Falsafa al-ʿArabiyya al-Islamiyya* (Materialist Tendencies in Arab-Islamic Philosophy), Muruwwa argued that materialist trends existed within classical Islamic thought itself.[9] Unlike al-ʿAzm and Tarabishi who viewed *turath* primarily through the lens of critique, Tuma and Muruwwa sought to uncover progressive elements within the tradition that could be mobilised for contemporary struggles.

---

4 Al-Jawzi 2015.

5 Al-Jawzi's ground-breaking application of Marxist methodology to Islamic historical analysis represented a significant epistemological shift in Arab historiography. His work preceded later materialist interpretations of Islamic history by several decades. For more about Al-Jawzi's work, see Sonn 1996.

6 For a detailed analysis of the different intellectual contexts of Palestinian scholarship under the British Mandate versus within Israel, see Pappe 2011.

7 Tarabishi 1982, p. 23.

8 Al-Azm 1968, pp. 78–9.

9 Muruwwa 1988, pp. 23–5.

The fundamental distinction between Tuma's approach and that of Al-ʿAzm and Tarabishi lies not merely in their conclusions about *turath*, but in their methodological orientations and epistemological frameworks, which reflected deeper disagreements about the relationship between tradition, reason, and social transformation.

Al-ʿAzm and Tarabishi's approach operated through what can be termed a hermeneutics of suspicion – they approached *turath* as an external object requiring systematic demystification. They employed analytical methods that positioned the critic outside the tradition to expose its ideological functions.[10] Al-ʿAzm's *Naqd al-Fikr al-Dini* (Critique of Religious Thought) (1968) systematically demonstrated how traditional religious concepts like *qadar* (divine predestination) functioned to legitimise social inequality and political authoritarianism by encouraging passive acceptance of existing conditions. Similarly, Tarabishi's psychoanalytic approach in *The Massacre of Heritage in Contemporary Arab Culture* diagnosed contemporary Arab engagement with *turath* as collective psychological regression – a retreat into historical nostalgia that avoided confronting modern challenges. Both scholars advocated complete epistemological rupture with traditional thought patterns, viewing any positive engagement with Islamic heritage as inherently regressive and incompatible with scientific rationality.

Tuma's materialist dialectics, by contrast, employed what can be described as immanent critique – a methodology that worked within the tradition to identify contradictory tendencies rather than dismissing it wholesale. This approach involved several distinctive analytical moves. First, Tuma practiced internal dialectical analysis, refusing to treat classic Islamic movements as monolithically progressive or reactionary. Instead, he demonstrated how the same historical formation – such as the Muʿtazila theological school – could simultaneously advance intellectual freedom through rational inquiry while serving imperial coercion when aligned with state power. Second, his class-based hermeneutics read religious movements as expressions of underlying social contradictions, analysing how different class positions produced different theological interpretations within Islam itself. Third, unlike Al-ʿAzm's rejection or Tarabishi's psychological critique, Tuma advocated strategic appropriation – selectively mobilising progressive elements from Islamic tradition for contemporary liberation struggles while maintaining critical distance from reactionary tendencies.

---

10 Kassab 2010, pp. 167–70.

This methodological distinction becomes clearer when comparing Tuma's approach with other contemporary intellectuals who were also seeking indigenous sources of radicalism, such as Ali Shariʿati. While Shariʿati, pursued similar projects, Tuma's specific contribution lay in his historically materialist methodology rather than in the general goal of cultural authenticity. Ali Shariʿati emphasised spiritual authenticity and Islamic identity against Western cultural imperialism, seeking to Islamicise revolutionary consciousness rather than secularise Islamic tradition. Shariʿati's approach focused on existential authenticity and psychological liberation from cultural alienation, developing what might be characterised as romantic nationalism that idealised both Persian identity and the early Islamic community.

Tuma's historical materialist innovation differed fundamentally from Shariʿati's cultural approach. Where Shariʿati sought authentic Islamic identity, Tuma applied systematic class analysis to pre-modern Islamic movements, developing periodisation frameworks that traced the material conditions behind theological developments. Rather than celebrating Islamic culture generally, Tuma created analytical tools for distinguishing between form and content in religious discourse – demonstrating how identical theological concepts could serve different class interests in different historical periods.

The scholarly significance of Tuma's intervention thus lay not in the general recognition that Islamic tradition contained resources for contemporary politics – a point acknowledged by diverse thinkers from Shariʿati to Muhammad Abduh – but in his development of indigenous Marxist historiography of Islamic civilisation. Unlike Shariʿati's project of Islamic authenticity or Al-ʿAzm's secular demystification, Tuma created analytical frameworks that could account for the dialectical complexity of religious movements as simultaneously spiritual and material phenomena. This methodological innovation enabled him to identify concrete historical mechanisms through which religious movements could embody progressive political potential while maintaining their religious character – a theoretical contribution that remains relevant for understanding contemporary Islamic movements beyond simplistic secular/religious binaries.[11]

Tuma's distinctive contribution to Marxist theory lay in developing what can be termed dialectical religious analysis. This involved three key methodological innovations. First, movement trajectory analysis traced how the same religious movement could evolve from progressive to reactionary character under changing material conditions – as demonstrated in his examination of how

11 Tuma 1978.

the Muʿtazila's rational theology transformed from intellectual liberation into imperial orthodoxy. Second, his class-religious synthesis showed how religious discourse simultaneously expressed spiritual concerns and material interests without reducing one to the other, challenging both reductionist Marxism that dismissed religion as false consciousness and idealist approaches that treated religious ideas as autonomous from material conditions. Third, his strategic appropriation theory developed criteria for distinguishing between progressive and reactionary elements within religious traditions for contemporary political use, providing practical guidance for leftist engagement with Islamic heritage.

This theoretical framework positioned Tuma's work as a significant intervention within Marxist discourse on religion and social change. Rather than simply applying existing Marxist categories to Islamic materials, Tuma developed a modified historical materialist methodology specifically adapted to societies where religious and political authority were institutionally integrated, where theological discourse served as the primary language for articulating social criticism, and where cultural tradition provided both resources for resistance and instruments of domination.

Tuma's analysis rested on a crucial theoretical insight that distinguished his approach from both conventional Marxist treatments of religion and traditional Islamic scholarship: his recognition that Islam's uniqueness lies in that it does not differentiate between the material world and theology.[12] This observation represented more than a descriptive claim about Islamic doctrine; it constituted a fundamental theoretical argument with significant implications for both historical analysis and contemporary political strategy.

The theoretical foundation of this argument lay in Tuma's analysis of the Prophetic model of social transformation established during the Medina period. Unlike religious movements that focused primarily on individual spiritual transformation or otherworldly salvation, the Prophet Muhammad's community created what Tuma characterised as integrated praxis where spiritual, political, and economic transformation occurred simultaneously. The Constitution of Medina established new social relations based on religious community (*umma*) rather than tribal affiliation, while simultaneously organising economic cooperation, political governance, and military defence. This historical precedent demonstrated that Islamic transformation was never purely 'spiritual' but always involved concrete material reorganisation of social relations.

This integration manifested in Islamic law and social institutions in ways that distinguished Islam from other major religious traditions. The Quran's

12 Tuma 1979a, p. 28.

detailed prescriptions regarding wealth distribution (*zakat*), commercial relations (prohibition of *riba*/usury), inheritance law, and social justice (*ʿadl*) integrated theological principles with economic practice in systematic fashion. Unlike Christianity's potential separation between rendering 'unto Caesar' and pursuing spiritual salvation, or Buddhism's emphasis on individual liberation from material attachments, Islam presented unified divine guidance for both spiritual development and material social organisation. The institutional expression of this unity appeared in the caliphate (*khilafa*), which functioned simultaneously as religious leadership implementing divine law and political authority governing material society.

The political significance of this material-theological integration became apparent in Tuma's analysis of Islamic social movements. Because religious discourse necessarily addressed material concerns, Islamic movements could articulate revolutionary social change without the alienation from worldly engagement that might characterise other religious traditions. The Qarmatian and Ismaʿili movements exemplified this potential, using theological language to organise radical economic reorganisation including collective property ownership and egalitarian social relations. Their revolutionary programs gained popular support precisely because they connected spiritual transformation with concrete material improvements in followers' lives.

For Marxist analysis, this integration required methodological modifications to standard historical materialist approaches. Mechanical applications of base-superstructure models, which treated religion as an ideological reflection of economic relations, could not account for societies where religious and economic institutions were systematically integrated. Islamic societies required analysis of religious discourse and examination of theological debates for their material subtext without reducing them to pure ideology, and evaluation of Islamic movements through their concrete social effects rather than their theological content alone.

This theoretical insight carried important implications for contemporary political strategy in Islamic societies. If Islam inherently connected spiritual and material transformation, then secular materialist discourse alone could not achieve cultural hegemony among populations whose worldview integrated religious and social concerns. Progressive politics would need to engage with Islamic tradition's material-theological unity rather than dismissing religion as false consciousness or attempting to confine it to private spiritual matters.

However, Tuma's analysis also revealed dialectical dangers inherent in this integration. The same unity that enabled revolutionary transformation could support religious authoritarianism if political power claimed divine legitimacy, making opposition appear as theological heresy rather than legitimate political dissent. Similarly, ruling classes could instrumentalise Islamic discourse to legitimise economic inequality and political oppression precisely because religion addressed material as well as spiritual concerns. Most problematically, because political conflicts necessarily involved theological interpretation, social struggles could take sectarian forms that divided potentially unified class movements along religious lines.

The contemporary relevance of this analysis extended beyond academic historiography to practical political challenges facing Leftist movements throughout the Islamic world. Tuma's recognition that Islam's material-theological unity made it both a potential resource for liberation and a possible instrument of domination provided analytical framework for understanding why Islamic discourse became central to anti-colonial movements, why secular nationalist projects often failed to achieve popular legitimacy, and why contemporary Islamic movements could articulate both progressive and reactionary political programs using similar theological language.

In addition, as we have seen, Emile Tuma's writings were not primarily concerned with purely academic analysis but were part of his partisan tasks, which were linked to the intellectual confrontations waged by the Communist Party in Israel in particular and the communist and socialist movement in the Arab and Islamic world in general, with the increasing weight of political Islam movements influenced on the one hand by the literature of the Muslim Brotherhood in Egypt and on the other hand by the victory of the Islamic Revolution in Iran.

CHAPTER 3

Survey of *Al-Harakat Al-Ijtimaʿiyya fi Al-Islam*

In his introductory chapter, Tuma divided his book into five parts, which include twelve chapters.

In the introductory chapter, Tuma highlights the significance of comprehending history and introduces his fundamental concepts regarding historical analysis. Tuma emphasises that using a modern perspective is not appropriate to judge past eras, especially in Islamic-Arab history. However, we can still distinguish between progressive and regressive or reactionary trends. This knowledge, he claimed, is essential in understanding the challenges faced by the Arab Liberation Movement in achieving revolutionary development.[1]

Tuma believed that a thorough understanding of Arab and Islamic history could help identify progressive forces that could be utilised in the modern era to liberate Arab nations from external colonialism. He aimed to uncover the intellectual and political currents within Islamic history that have been suppressed to rediscover this heritage's revolutionary potential and eliminate the reactionary forces associated with it.[2]

In the first chapter of his book, Tuma emphasises the importance of his research's primary theme, which is religion's role in overall social progress. Throughout this chapter, Tuma makes broad observations regarding the role religion plays in the development of societies. He aims to answer whether religion is the driving force behind societal development, as some researchers suggest, or if it reflects deeper factors such as social, economic, and historical changes in a specific region of the world.[3]

As a Marxist, Tuma asserts that religions, with their differences, are all reflections of certain historical developments in historical periods in themselves that led to the emergence of these religions and their domination of the human imagination to the extent that people have come to believe that religion itself is the engine of history, which Tuma categorically rejects.

In this chapter, Tuma discusses the three major religions, Buddhism, Christianity, and Islam, that have attracted millions of followers. He highlights

1 Tuma 1979, p. 13.
2 Tuma 1979, p. 15.
3 Tuma 1979, p. 28.

 | HTTPS://DOI.ORG/10.1163/9789004774261-004

Islam's uniqueness in that it does not differentiate between the material world and theology. This feature sets Islam apart and requires careful consideration by historians and materialist researchers studying intellectual and social movements that have emerged within the Islamic context.[4]

In the next chapter, Tuma discusses the role of religion in human history. He then proceeds to lay the groundwork for social ideas in Islam, starting with its first source. Tuma presents a drawing of the pre-Islamic social conflict between two groups of the *Quraysh* tribe and the alliances that were formed by these groups. He explains how Mecca's unique geographical location played a crucial role in elevating its status among Arab tribes inhabiting the Arabian Peninsula. This location became the ideal centre for the new movement that would unite the Arab tribes and bring about a shift from tribalism to a united nation, known as the *umma*.[5]

In this chapter, Tuma argues that the roots of class conflict and social justice can be traced back to the very beginning of Islam. He connects this to the surrounding human and material conditions of the time. Tuma highlights that Prophet Muhammad belonged to a less affluent group that was in opposition to the wealthier group in Mecca. As a result, the 'material reality' of this situation found its way into the religious and social consciousness of Islam during its early years.[6]

It is important to note that Tuma, just as al-Jawzi before him, does not categorise Islam as inherently 'socialist'. Instead, he focuses on two key aspects that can lay the foundation for progressive ideals within Islam. Firstly, the Quran acknowledges the existence of class differences and the resulting class struggle. Secondly, there is a call for social justice to be implemented to ensure fairness among different social groups. While this has not yet led to the complete elimination of private property in society, it could serve as a starting point to achieve this goal in the future, according to Tuma.

Then, Tuma shifts his focus from theology and metaphysics to the earthly reality of Islamic history. He discusses the first political conflict in Islam after the death of the Prophet and how this conflict is connected to previous conflicts. The conflict is not solely based on mechanical concepts or conflicting tribes, but rather on defining the interests of each party involved in the struggle. Tuma explores the causes and underlying currents that drive these conflicts.

---

4 Ibid.

5 Tuma 1979, pp. 35–8.

6 Tuma 1979, p. 42; Salih 1973, pp. 30–1.

While traditional historians tend to focus on the *saqifa* incident and the debate between the *al-ansar*[7] and *al-muhajirun*[8] as groups with varying origins and affiliations to Mecca and Yathrib, Tuma like other Marxist historians[9] who analyse history through a materialistic lens see the discussion and its outcome as a clash between different social forces within the young Islamic state. According to this perspective, the selection of Abu Bakr Al-Siddiq (573–634) and ʿUmar Ibn Al-Khattab (586?–644) as leaders represented the victory of the Islamic 'centre' party over the 'right' and 'left' factions, which would later manifest in the caliphates of ʿUthman (576–656) and ʿAli (600–61). Eventually, the 'right' faction would gain dominance with Muʿawiyah's rise to power and the formation of a monarchy, which marked the end of the *shura* (consultative) democracy that had been in its early stages during this period.[10]

Tuma believes that the emergence of Shiism is rooted in a political bias towards ʿAli Ibn Abi Talib and his representation of the social positions of the left. The left-wing interpretation of Islam views it as a religion for the poor and working classes, rather than favouring the wealthy or aristocratic classes as represented by the Shura Committee appointed by ʿUmar ibn al-Khattab before his death. Out of the six members on the committee, five were from the wealthy class of Mecca, including Uthman ibn Affan, Abd al-Rahman ibn Awf (580–656), Saʿd ibn Abi Waqqas (595?–674), Talha (594–656), and al-Zubayr (594–656), all of whom were wealthy members of Quraish. Ali ibn Abi Talib was the only member with a different orientation, and according to Tuma, the committee could not choose him for succession. As a result, it was natural for the committee to choose ʿUthman, a member of their own class.[11]

Tuma believes that Shia represents the dominant religious beliefs of the opposing factions within the Islamic empire. These groups, who have faced discrimination based on factors such as social class, nationality, race, and language, have united under the banner of supporting the Prophet's family and Ali's descendants. The popularity of Ismailism and its various offshoots has been fuelled by their ability to mobilise support among the common people.[12]

---

7 The helpers, or 'Ansar', were the local inhabitants of Medina who welcomed the *muhajirun* and also became Muslims, joining the Umma.

8 The first Muslims emigrated from Mecca to Medina with the Prophet Muhammad.

9 See, for example, Bandali al-Jawzi's *The Intellectual Movements in Islam*; Anwar Khatib's *The Socialist Trend in Islam; and* Ahmad Abbas Salih's *The Right and the Left in Islam.*

10 Salih 1973, p. 58.

11 Tuma 1979, p. 60.

12 Tuma 1979, p. 73.

Tuma extensively discussed revolutionary movements that had a Shiite aspect, each with its own unique characteristics. Within the fourth chapter of his book, he delved into the intricacies of the Ismaili movement, examining its implications and the varying perspectives of the Fatimids and Qarmatians. He highlights the apparent contradiction between two aspects of these movements. On one hand, their revolutionary tendencies and ability to attract popular classes, as well as the establishment of some social ownership over the means of production. On the other hand, the development of an exaggerated concept of alignment towards the Imam and the cultivation of pious and esoteric ideas. These ideas emerged in response to the injustices and abuses of rights experienced in the early stages of the movement. Tuma, like other Marxist writers, seeks to explain the various positions of these movements by grounding them in their historical, materialistic, and realistic foundations, rather than in an idealistic struggle between intellectual currents that are disconnected from their concrete social and economic reality.[13]

He adopts a similar approach to handle the 'rational' movement in Islam, known as the Muʿtazila. In the chapter that elaborates on the Muʿtazila, Tuma clarifies their philosophical views and portrays their political development during the Umayyad period (661–750). At this time, the economic prosperity of the Islamic middle class, merchants, and landowners resulted in significant contact with philosophical currents from the East (including Indian philosophies) and the West (including Greek philosophers). This led to a conflict that made them seek reconciliation between religion and reason. They developed interpretation mechanisms for the Quran and the Prophet's hadiths to achieve the closest statements that align with their fundamental positions (especially class), while also being compatible with religion and not contradicting it.[14]

Tuma argues that Muʿtazilite thought was stuck in its own inertia, leading them to attribute matters to the matters' selves rather than their socio-economic context. The ideal positions of the Muʿtazilites are considered part of the intellectual thought development of their period, but their inability to overcome their class position meant that these ideas became the views of the ruling class and the official ideology of the state during the period of al-Ma'mun in the Abbasid state. The Muʿtazila, who were once a progressive intellectual force, became a tool of repression against those who opposed them. This period in Islamic history is known as the *mihna* (ordeal) for anyone who opposed the

13 Tuma 1979, pp. 75–7.

14 Tuma 1979, p. 92.

official Muʿtazilite approach, especially in the issue of creating the Quran. The Muʿtazilites believed that the Qur'an was created and not eternal, which was in opposition to the beliefs of most Muslims.

During the reign of Caliph al-Mutawakkil (ruled 847–61), the feudal system reached its zenith. Tuma believed that this system required an ideological representation distinct from the Muʿtazila. As a result, the Ashʿari thought emerged, which aimed to re-establish the immutable Islamic texts and the more conservative interpretations of religious texts. This led to the suppression of progressive interpretations that supported freedom, and the intellectual debates that flourished during the Muʿtazila era were closed off.[15]

Tuma believed that Abu Hassan al-Ashʿari's ideas were based on two types of factors: the 'objective' factor, which was the explosion of social revolutions within the Islamic state through the Zanj (slaves from Africa) and Qarmatian revolutions. These revolutions aimed to promote social equality within the Abbasid society, resulting in the need to prevent liberal ideas through a philosophical vision that curbs freedom of thought. This vision emphasises that the status quo and class inequality are nothing but 'fate and destiny' and God's will on earth.

But Abu Hassan Al-Ashʿari's (874–936) reactionary equation was also, influenced by a subjective factor, as per Tuma. It was his incapability to keep up with the philosophical debates of the Muʿtazilites. Therefore, he sought to shut down these discussions with Islamic fundamentalist beliefs, prioritising the text over the realisation of reason and thought.[16]

In chapter seven of the book, Tuma sheds light on one of the most problematic and harmful movements from the perspective of 'orthodox Islam'. This movement is known as 'shuʿubiyya' from the outset. However, Tuma is hesitant to consider shuʿubiyya as a movement, but rather as a tendency that has not evolved into a mass movement capable of uniting popular forces.

According to Tuma's analytical and 'objective' reading of history, shuʿubiyya can be divided into two phases. In the first phase, shuʿubiyya was a progressive movement that aimed to establish equality between the Arabs and other Islamic peoples within the vast Islamic state. It sought to counter Arab fanaticism that had reached its peak during the Umayyad rule. Tuma believed that the arrival of the Abbasids to power and the Persians' support for them caused shuʿubiyya to gradually become more reactionary, expressing anti-Arab racism during its second phase. Additionally, Tuma argued that the civil war between

15 Tuma 1979, p. 105.

16 Tuma 1979, pp. 113–4.

the two brothers Al-Amin (ruled 809–13) (supported by Arab forces) and Al-Ma'moun (r. 813–33) (supported by the Persians) resulted in the victory of Al-Ma'moun and the domination of the shuʿubiyya. This tendency became part of the intellectual framework of the ruling class in the Abbasid state, shifting it from a progressive to a reactionary and racist tendency that works to maintain the existing class distribution in the state.

Tuma concludes that shuʿubiyya positively impacted curbing Arab nationalist fanaticism and promoting a climate that supported the growth of social and revolutionary movements. This was particularly evident in the Qarmatian movement and the Zanj revolution, which rejected Arab fanaticism and the existing status quo. Shuʿubiyya played a significant role in this regard, even though these movements were not directly related to it.[17]

In the eighth chapter, Tuma moves to give an overview of the relationship between religion and nationalism in general with his refutation of the fact that religion and nationalism are two different stages in history. Tuma considered that religion and nationalism have interacted with each other throughout history. Even before nationalism matured to its current developed concept, which Tuma brings back to the bourgeois stage. He argues that embryonic nationalist tendencies existed in ancient history. The modern nationalist movements also built, among other things, their legitimacy on religious consensus among members of the same people, and he brings examples from Europe and other parts of the world.[18]

In the next chapter, Tuma shifts his focus to the Arab world to explore the organic connection between religion and nationalism among the different Arab communities. He examines the emergence of Arab nationalism as a progressive force that challenged the Ottoman authorities' efforts to exploit religion to hold onto their Turkish dominance over the majority of the Ottoman Empire's populations, especially the Arabs.[19]

Tuma observed two parallel trends in the Arab world- an Islamic trend and a nationalist trend. The Ottomans adopted Islam as their slogan, using religious slogans to cover their oppression of the Arabs and Arabism, particularly in the Levant and Iraq. This manipulation strengthened the nationalist trend in these countries. The idea of the Islamic league and pan-Islamism of Sultan Abdul Hamid II was also used to manipulate religious slogans. Meanwhile, the Maghreb countries were distant from Ottoman oppression and instead were under European colonial occupation. This mitigated the clash between the Islamic

17 Tuma 1979, p. 133.
18 Tuma 1979, pp. 135–49.
19 Tuma 1979, p. 151.

and nationalist trends, resulting in their mixing. The Maghreb nationalist trend had a strong Islamic spirit, as it was facing European colonialists who used Crusader slogans to justify their occupation.[20]

In Chapter Ten, Tuma discusses the issue of sectarianism. He focuses on how sectarian differences are exploited to incite conflicts among different sects and how this leads to a fragmentation of national and patriotic groups in various countries. His main interest lies in the Levant region, (which includes Syria, Lebanon, Palestine, and Transjordan), and Egypt.

Tuma argues that sectarianism is a product of feudalism in certain countries, which aimed to maintain their power by dividing people along sectarian lines. This prevented the popular classes from uniting against the feudal lords. Tuma cites several examples, including the conflicts between the Druze and Maronite feudal lords in Mount Lebanon, as well as the disputes between the popular communes of these two sects. Additionally, Tuma emphasises the role of imperial powers in exacerbating sectarian tensions. These powers attempted to gain influence by aligning themselves with one of the minority sects within the Ottoman Empire. For instance, France supported the Maronites and Catholics, Tsarist Russia supported the Orthodox, and Britain supported the Druze in Mount Lebanon. This was often done under the pretext of protecting these groups, even though their true motives were to establish their own foothold in the region.

In the final chapter of the book, Tuma discusses the period following Turkish colonialism and the Ottoman Empire, when British and French colonialism was dominant in the Arab Levant region. He emphasises how the colonial powers exploited sectarian divisions to divide and control the people.

Tuma particularly emphasises France's attempt to divide Greater Syria into different sectarian states, and the partial failure of this attempt. While his book concludes with a few lines about the ruling authority in the State of Israel inheriting the 'divide and rule' approach in order to control the Palestinian Arab nationalist minority inside Israel by trying to separate the Arab Druze community from the rest of the Arab masses. At the same time, it confirms the failure of these policies.[21]

20 Tuma 1979, pp. 151–2.

21 Tuma 1979, p. 190.

PART 2

Social Movements in Islam, by Emile Tuma

Translated by Ruba Simaan
Edited and annotated by Abed Kanaaneh

PREFACE

Understanding History

In his eulogy for Karl Marx, Friedrich Engels remarked by Marx's graveside:

> Just as Darwin discovered the law of development of organic nature, so Marx discovered the law of development of human history: the simple fact, hitherto concealed by an overgrowth of ideology, that mankind must first of all eat, drink, have shelter and clothing, before it can pursue politics, science, art, religion, etc.; that therefore the production of the immediate material means, and consequently the degree of economic development attained by a given people or during a given epoch, form the foundation upon which the state institutions, the legal conceptions, art, and even the ideas on religion, of the people concerned have been evolved ...[1]

Marx aimed to articulate the essence of his historical materialism as follows:

> In the social production of their existence, men inevitably enter into definite relations, which are independent of their will, namely relations of production appropriate to a given stage in the development of their material forces of production. The totality of these relations of production constitutes the economic structure of society, the real foundation, on which arises a legal and political superstructure and to which correspond definite forms of social consciousness. The mode of production of material life conditions the general process of social, political and intellectual life. It is not the consciousness of men that determines their existence, but their social existence that determines their consciousness.[2]

Given the framework of Marxist historical materialism, Engels articulated the interpretation of social reality as follows:

> But the old idealist conception of history, which was not yet dislodged, knew nothing of class struggles based upon economic interests, knew nothing of economic interests; production and all economic relations appeared in it only as incidental, subordinate elements in the 'history of civilisation'. The new facts

1 Engels 1883.
2 Marx 1859.

 | HTTPS://DOI.ORG/10.1163/9789004774261-005

> made imperative a new examination of all past history. Then it was seen that *all* past history was the history of class struggles; that these warring classes of society are always the products of the modes of production and of exchange – in a word, of the *economic* conditions of their time.[3]

Therefore, it is accurate to assert that history began with Marx, who uncovered the laws governing societal development. In doing so, he challenged the idealist perspectives that had subjected history to chaotic theories and portrayed historical events as a mere confluence of accidents and spontaneous occurrences.

However, the clarity provided by the laws of societal development did not resolve all historical issues. Significant challenges emerged due to misunderstandings of historical materialism and its application in a mechanistic manner. This situation compelled Engels, who assumed responsibility for safeguarding the integrity of Marxism after Karl Marx's death, to ardently defend it as the definitive guide for historical research, rather than a Hegelian construct based on Hegel's concept of the Absolute. Engels emphasised this point in his book, stating that 'there is a certain order in nature and history that encompasses and determines the end of everything, thus contradicting the fundamental principles of dialectical thinking. However, this does not prevent but rather necessitates that organised knowledge of the external world advances significantly from one generation to the next'.[4]

On these grounds, Marx and Engels proposed a general theory of human history, positing that primitive communism was the predominant social system in early societies, succeeded by capitalism. They anticipated that capitalism, being the final class-based regime, would be followed by socialism, which represents the initial stage of a classless communist society. The validation of their theory was demonstrated by the success of the socialist revolution in Tsarist Russia, with its flags now waving triumphantly over vast regions in Asia, Europe, Africa and Latin America, where hundreds of millions of people reside.

These general guidelines provide a framework for understanding the development of history, examining its various stages, and appreciating its notable figures. However, they cannot serve as a universal key for analysing Arab history, understanding its stages, and recognising its prominent figures. Instead,

3 Engels 1877.

4 Tuma provides neither the title of the work nor the precise page reference for this citation. (A.K.)

these guidelines should be viewed as a tool for illuminating the path and establishing objective foundations for examining the unique national characteristics that must be acknowledged due to their significance and alignment with the principles of human historical development.

It is evident that Arab history is divided into distinct stages, with class conflict persisting throughout all phases following primitive communism or tribal regimes. When analysing these stages, it is crucial to refer to historical materialism and align with Stalin's assertion that:

> All social systems and movements in history should not be evaluated based on the notion of 'eternal justice' or predefined ideas, as historians often do. Instead, they should be assessed in the context of the circumstances in which a particular social system or movement emerged.[5]

Therefore, it is misguided to judge ancient times by contemporary standards or to apply modern social and political values to societies with different economic bases and types of economic relations.

For example, the Umayyad Caliphate,[6] when assessed within the context of its time, represented a notable development beyond the Rashidun[7] era, despite its shortcomings by modern standards. While the early Rashidun Caliphs – excluding Othman bin Affan – sought to promote social justice during the initial phase of the Arab conquests and the formation of the Empire, the Umayyads introduced a distinct political order that reflected the evolving needs of a growing imperial structure. Similarly, the Zanj Rebellion,[8] though ultimately unsuccessful in dismantling the class hierarchy, should be understood as an expression of class struggle within its historical constraints. Rather than a transformative force, it served as an early indicator of class tensions that had yet to mature into a broader societal shift.

---

5 Tuma provides neither the title of the work nor the precise page reference for this citation. (A.K.)

6 The Umayyad Caliphate (661–750 CE) was the second of the four major Islamic caliphates, ruling from Damascus and overseeing vast territorial expansion across the Middle East, North Africa, and into the Iberian Peninsula, while establishing lasting administrative structures in the Islamic world. (A.K.)

7 The Rashidun Caliphate (632–61 CE) was the first Islamic caliphate, ruled by the four 'Rightly-Guided Caliphs' (Abu Bakr, Umar, Uthman, and Ali) who were direct companions of Prophet Muhammad and oversaw the initial expansion of Islam beyond the Arabian Peninsula. (A.K.)

8 The Zanj Rebellion (869–83 CE) was a major slave revolt in southern Iraq led by enslaved East Africans working in the salt marshes near Basra, who under the leadership of Ali ibn Muhammad established an independent state that lasted fourteen years before being suppressed by Abbasid forces. (A.K.)

In this regard, Marx asserted that:

> No social order is ever destroyed before all the productive forces for which it is sufficient have been developed, and new superior relations of production never replace older ones before the material conditions for their existence have matured within the framework of the old society.[9]

This assertion is particularly relevant. This societal development law suggests that the Qarmatian Revolution should be judged according to the standards of the period, leading to the conclusion that the circumstances at that time were not conducive to the eradication of Arab-Islamic feudalism[10] that prevailed during the era.

Although we don't evaluate historical eras by the standards of our times, it is essential to examine them through the lens of our intellectual concepts and Marxist philosophy. Marxist philosophy itself is a product of our contemporary era, as its emergence was necessitated by the current epoch. Our time has witnessed the rise of the modern proletariat, which, according to the laws of societal development, is tasked with the mission of abolishing class structures and establishing socialism, followed eventually by communism.

Thus, we analyse history from a class-based perspective and assess ancient periods from a proletarian viewpoint, which starkly contrasts with and often

---

9 Marx 1859.

10 Tuma's terminological choices require careful contextualisation within 1970s Arab Marxist historiography. His analytical framework reflects the influence of Soviet historical materialism, particularly scholars such as V.B. Lutsky, evident in his application of concepts like 'feudalism' to diverse Islamic social formations. However, Tuma demonstrated awareness of the distinctions between European feudal concepts and their Islamic historical counterparts, recognising the different conditions governing each social system, as evidenced by his observations on this methodological problem on page 111. While such terminology reflected the theoretical apparatus available to scholars of his generation, it occasionally obscured the distinctive historical particularities of Islamic societies. This conceptual approach characterised much Marxist historiography of the period, as scholars endeavoured to integrate diverse historical experiences within broader theoretical frameworks. Contemporary scholars seeking alternative approaches to the question of 'feudalism' in classical Islamic social formations may find Rodinson's complementary perspectives valuable, as his work demonstrates how historical materialist analysis can accommodate the specific contours of Islamic historical development. Rodinson's contribution illustrates how Islamic societies developed distinctive political economies that necessitate modifications to European historical categories rather than their wholesale rejection. (A.K.)

contradicts the bourgeois perspective. While we address various historical systems and concepts within their temporal context, it is crucial not to separate these from their class foundations. For instance, when examining the Zanj Rebellion or the Qarmatian Revolution, our evaluation extends beyond their historical context and the societal phase in which they occurred. We interpret these events as heroic struggles initiated by labourers, despite their inability to achieve success.

In this regard, we diverge from bourgeois historians who, when evaluating these revolutions, do so from a bourgeois perspective, often dismissing them as delusions or chaos. It is no coincidence that historians from the Abbasid Caliphate who witnessed the Zanj Rebellion referred to its leader pejoratively, a sentiment echoed by bourgeois contemporary authors. One such author described the Zanj Rebellion as 'having escalated during al-Muʿtazz's reign, led by an Iranian man who allowed his followers to commit egregious transgressions'.[11]

Given that the history of human society is fundamentally a history of class conflict and drawing inspiration from the interests of the modern working class, which is tasked by historical laws with the mission of eradicating class structures, we inherently portray the struggles of the working class throughout history as heroic endeavours. These struggles are assessed according to contemporary standards while remaining mindful of their historical context. It is crucial to avoid misrepresenting their true nature; rather, we should recognise their real limitations and strive for a realistic understanding of the historical stage within the framework of societal development.

Hence, while we rightly recognise the bourgeois revolution in Britain as a major progressive step, having dismantled feudalism and given rise to the modern proletariat, we also celebrate the uprising of the Levellers (advocates of social rank equality) as the revolutionary expression of a class whose formation was still incomplete. This movement, though embryonic, embodied the early stirrings of a class that, once fully developed, holds the potential to overthrow the bourgeoisie and abolish the class system altogether. We regard them as the vanguard of the class destined to achieve the socialist revolution, much like we see the Zanj as pioneers of the inevitably victorious modern proletariat.

When discussing past notions and views, we do so from contemporary perspectives, evaluating them by modern standards within their historical context.

11 Ali 1938 [1924], no page number cited.

This allows us to classify some of these ideas as progressive and others as reactionary. For example, we consider utopian socialists like Saint-Simon, Fourier, and Robert Owen (all of whom preceded Karl Marx) to be progressive relative to their time. They made significant discoveries and called for utopian socialism after condemning abusive capitalism. They are seen as the pioneers of socialism and proposed ideas that align well with our current standards. Fourier, for instance, was the first to assert that the level of women's liberation measures a society's level of liberation.

Therefore, while we judge concepts within their specific historical contexts, we acknowledge that certain ideas represent emerging forces and are progressive relative to their era. Some of these concepts and perspectives were significantly ahead of their time and should be evaluated based on the overall historical development rather than by the standards of their own period. Engels, for example, wrote that 'The real progenitor of English materialism is Bacon. To him, natural philosophy is the only true philosophy, and physics based upon the experience of the senses is the chiefest part of natural philosophy'.[12] It is crucial to have a clear understanding and accurate measure when examining intellectual heritage. We must select from this heritage those progressive elements that have contributed significantly to cultural development while rejecting reactionary beliefs, even if we recognise that these beliefs are derived from a particular economic basis and constitute its main super-structure.

For example, we choose to highlight Abu al-ʿAla' al-Maʿarri[13] because he carried the torch of materialist philosophy and ridiculed the irrational superstitions prevalent in his time, rather than al-Ghazali,[14] who, despite his intellectual stature, represented a reactionary philosophical orientation. We commend al-Maʿarri for his materialist outlook, his advocacy of inter-sectarian tolerance, and the depth of his political thought – particularly in rejecting the notion of a singular savior or leader as the solution to societal ills. However, we do not praise his views on women, even though we understand them as reflective of the dominant attitudes of the ruling class in his era, rather than of the perspectives that would emerge among subsequent social strata.

---

12 Engels 1880 (A.K.)

13 Abu al-ʿAla' al-Maʿarri (973–1057 CE) was a Syrian poet and philosopher, known for his skeptical and rationalist views, as well as his influential works in Arabic literature that questioned religious dogma and social conventions. (A.K.)

14 Al-Ghazali (1058–1111 CE) was a Persian theologian, jurist, philosopher, and mystic of the Islamic Golden Age, whose works, including *Ihya' ʿUlum al-Din*, profoundly influenced Sunni Islamic thought, integrating Sufism with orthodox Islamic theology. (A.K.)

The question of how to present and interpret the ideas of classical intellectual figures is never abstract or ahistorical; it is shaped by the temporal and spatial context in which it arises and is always embedded within the framework of contemporary historical conditions and the dynamics of ongoing political struggles.

For instance, emphasising the Arabism of Al-Mutanabbi[15] is crucial, given that he celebrated his people amidst the intensifying Arab struggle for freedom and independence. This approach does not distort history or judge Al-Mutanabbi by current standards; rather, it involves selecting aspects of his work that resonate with the struggles of our era. His poetry echoes the enduring quest for liberation from foreign domination.

In essence, Al-Mutanabbi, as an Arab poet, used his Arabic poetry to articulate his nation's aspiration to free itself from external control, reflecting a continuity of struggle across centuries.

Some persist in the view that nationalism is a modern phenomenon that emerged solely under bourgeois conditions, overlooking the fact that modern nationalist movements have deep historical roots extending across the centuries. Arab history itself bears witness to the vitality of nationalist impulses during the period of the Arab Empire. Classical historians often described these movements as '*shuʿubiyya*', but this label does not alter their essential character: they were, in effect, nationalist movements – whether Persian, Georgian, Turkmen, or others.

Engels, Marx's close associate, remarked – while discussing the dawn of Islam in a letter to Marx – that:

> It is evident that the expulsion of the Abyssinians [from Yemen], which occurred forty years before Muhammad, marked the first chapter in the awakening of Arab national consciousness, an awakening spurred by Persian invasions from the north that nearly reached Mecca.[16]

If Engels identified the stirrings of Arab national awareness as predating both Islam and the Arab conquests, then are we mistaken in viewing al-Mutanabbi as a poet of Arab nationalism, or in evaluating his poetry through the lens

---

15 Al-Mutanabbi (915–65 CE) was a renowned Arab poet of the Abbasid period, celebrated for his eloquent and sophisticated poetry that combined personal ambition, political commentary, and philosophical reflection; his works later became a source of inspiration for Arab nationalist thought, as his emphasis on Arab identity and pride resonated with modern movements advocating Arab unity and cultural revival. (A.K.)

16 Complete bibliographic details not provided in Tuma's original citation. (A.K.)

of national struggle? Indeed, what fault lies in foregrounding al-Mutanabbi's Arabness in the present moment, when that very aspect offers inspiration to the ongoing struggles of the Arab people?

This is precisely the position to be taken regarding Shaykh Zahir al-ʿUmar.[17] This Arab feudal lord, who resisted Ottoman control, garnered the support of the Arab population in the region, and his movement, despite the historical conditions of the time, assumed a rudimentary nationalist character. Feudal conflicts can acquire a nationalist dimension when they oppose a local feudal power to a foreign autocracy. Yet, it is not sufficient to assert that the reactionary or progressive nature of an idea or a system depends solely on specific historical conditions; we must further acknowledge that the same idea can be reactionary or progressive depending on the historical context in which it arises. This nuanced assessment applies with full force to nationalist movements in our own time.

Nationalist movements in Africa, Asia, and Latin America that strive for independence from British or French colonial rule are inherently progressive and liberatory. These movements aim to extricate themselves from the domination of colonial powers that exploit and plunder their resources while oppressing their people. By seeking to end this foreign exploitation, these nationalist efforts represent a fundamental quest for self-determination and liberation.

In contrast, nationalist movements seeking separation from the Soviet Union or the People's Republic of China present a different dynamic. Such movements, under the guise of nationalism, often undermine the very national interests they purport to advance. Separating from a union of socialist states or from a specific socialist state can, in practice, lead to the restoration of capitalism and the re-subjugation of the working class. This shift not only betrays the original revolutionary goals but also risks reversing historical progress by reintroducing capitalist exploitation and diminishing the gains made under socialist governance. Thus, while the former movements represent a genuine struggle for liberation, the latter may, paradoxically, contribute to a regressive turn in the historical trajectory.

The essential task in understanding history lies in grasping the dialectic of development and recognising the role of contradictions, for, as Lenin stated, 'development is the struggle of opposites'.

---

17 Zahir al-ʿUmar al-Zaydani (1689/90–1775), Arab ruler who established virtually autonomous control over northern Palestine and the Galilee region in the mid-18th century, with his capital at Acre. He successfully resisted Ottoman authority for over 25 years and is considered a Palestinian national hero. (A.K.)

Marx demonstrated the depth of his dialectical philosophy in his analysis of British rule in India, identifying its dual function: destruction and regeneration. On the one hand, colonial rule dismantled the traditional social structures that had hindered India's economic progress; on the other, it inadvertently set in motion the emergence of new forces capable of building a modern economic society. In other words, Marx perceived both the negative and positive dimensions of British colonialism. This should not be misunderstood as an endorsement of the British occupation or as viewing it as inherently progressive, but rather as an expression of Marx's method of analysing historical reality through the lens of internal contradictions and the dialectics of development.

Undoubtedly, British colonialism dismantled existing structures and introduced new dynamics that ultimately contributed to the expulsion of the colonisers from India. As Marx noted, while colonialism was historically inevitable under the conditions of that era, it remained a system that the Indian people were justified in resisting, even by violent means. The Indian struggle, therefore, received the support of progressive humanity, which rightfully condemned the darker aspects of British colonialism and the associated barbarity of exploiting India's vast resources.

Thus, a comprehensive historical analysis requires a macro perspective – seeing the whole rather than the part and recognising the forces capable of advancing humanity rather than those that impede it. This approach makes the study of history both straightforward and challenging: it is straightforward because the laws of development are clear and provide guidance, yet challenging because applying these laws necessitates a nuanced understanding of both personal and general development and their organic interconnections.

CHAPTER 1

The Role of Religion in General Societal Development

Recent events have heightened scholarly interest in the intersections of religion and sectarianism, particularly as they have been implicated in the bloodshed witnessed in Northern Ireland, where Catholics and Protestants have clashed.[1] Similarly, Lebanon experienced the tragic civil war, often attributed to sectarian and religious tensions, even though the underlying causes were not solely religious or sectarian. This study seeks to address a pivotal question: What role does religion play in contemporary societal development?

Numerous rigorous studies have examined the role of religion in socio-political development. For instance, notable works addressing the relationship between religion and materialism include Werner Sombart's *The Jews and Modern Capitalism*, R.H. Tawney's *Religion and the Rise of Capitalism*, and Maxime Rodinson's *Islam and Capitalism*.[2]

A primary challenge for researchers is determining the approach used to define the relationship between religion and social and political developments. Two major approaches have emerged: the first posits that religion serves as

1 The reference to 'recent events' in Northern Ireland likely pertains to The Troubles, a period of ethno-nationalist conflict that intensified dramatically in the 1970s. Key incidents include Bloody Sunday (1972), when British paratroopers killed 14 unarmed Catholic civilians during a civil rights march, and the subsequent escalation of violence between republican paramilitaries (primarily the Provisional IRA), loyalist groups, and British security forces. The decade witnessed over 2,000 conflict-related deaths, making it the most violent period of The Troubles. While fundamentally a political conflict over Northern Ireland's constitutional status, the violence often manifested along Catholic-Protestant community lines, explaining scholarly interest in the intersection of religious identity and sectarian conflict.

2 Werner Sombart's *The Jews and Modern Capitalism* (1911) argued that Jewish cultural values shaped modern capitalism, though the work is now critiqued for essentialist assumptions and antisemitic stereotypes. R.H. Tawney's *Religion and the Rise of Capitalism* (1926) examined how Protestant ethics influenced capitalist development, building on Weber's "Protestant work ethic" thesis. Maxime Rodinson's *Islam and Capitalism* (1966) challenged orientalist assumptions by demonstrating Islam's historical compatibility with capitalist practices. Together, these works represent different approaches to understanding how religious worldviews intersect with economic systems. (A.K.)

 | HTTPS://DOI.ORG/10.1163/9789004774261-006

a foundational basis for societal development and political systems, with examples seen in the spread of Christianity and Islam during transitional historical periods. The second approach views religion as a component of the superstructure, reflecting significant changes within the society's socio-political infrastructure.

It is evident that all religions emerged within specific geographical regions and tangible social environments. Some of these environments have vanished entirely, while others have extended beyond their original boundaries, with very few achieving global significance.

This raises the question: Have religions determined the trajectory of human development and the successive socio-economic structures within human societies?

Examining primitive societies, which transitioned from a 'savagery' phase to a 'civilisation' phase, suggests that religions mirrored and reinforced the socio-economic developments of their time. Let us take, for instance, the *totem* – one of the earliest forms of religion in primitive communal societies. Totemism was shaped by the conditions of the rudimentary economy, which relied on hunting and gathering, and was grounded in blood relations among members of the community. The totemic belief rested on the idea that the deity was the ancestor of the believers, encompassing both the pure and the impure among the living.

This form of religion did not foster social or political advancements but rather solidified the existing situation and philosophy (if it can be termed so), further entrenching the practices and defining human relationships derived from emerging economic relations. The *Totem* system was associated with *Taboo*, which regulated sexual relationships to meet social needs and prohibited sexual relations between groups for the purposes of family planning.

However, this example, along with others from the transitions to civilisation in Ancient Egypt, Hellenistic Greece, and Buddhist India, does not fully address the core question we raised: Have religions subsequently shaped the path of development? The German philosopher Feuerbach, a contemporary of Karl Marx and Friedrich Engels – who formulated scientific communism and defined materialist philosophy – argued that different historical phases of humanity are primarily characterised by religious changes.

Friedrich Engels responded to this claim, asserting that such an assessment is fundamentally inaccurate – even though major historical turning points were indeed accompanied by the emergence of three world religions that have endured to this day: Buddhism, Christianity, and Islam. He added that tribal and national religions, which arose spontaneously, neither preached universal doctrines nor sought to win converts. As a result, they lost their capacity for resistance once the tribe lost its independence.[3]

Considering this, we can trace the emergence of the three religions: Buddhism emerged in India during the sixth century BCE, a period marked by the dismantling of primitive communal structures on the one hand, and the consolidation of a rigidly stratified class system – epitomised by the Brahmanical order – on the other. In this context, Buddhism represented a form of popular protest against Brahmanism, which had articulated the ethical and doctrinal foundations of the caste-based social order.[4] However, while Buddhism voiced discontent with the prevailing system, it did not advocate for social struggle; rather, it promoted spiritual liberation as the path to emancipation.

This indicates that Buddhism did not call for the alleviation of class-based oppression through social transformation but instead sought moral perfection through withdrawal from society and the renunciation of bodily desires and material ambitions. *Nirvana*, in this framework, was the Buddhist path to complete purity and union with the divine. Nevertheless, Buddhism eventually became the religion of ruling classes outside India, and to this day remains the faith of hundreds of millions across Asia, having long transcended its original geographic and social boundaries.

However, despite its social roots, ethical standards, spiritual values, and the practices of its leading figures, Buddhism did not ultimately determine the social systems that prevailed in significant regions of Asia. Over time, it began adapting to the successive social systems in certain nations where Buddhism is practiced to this day.

Christianity emerged six centuries after Buddhism, specifically in Palestine, one of the provinces of the expansive Roman Empire in the second half of the first century CE. It arose within the context of Jewish traditions but outside the framework of 'official Judaism', where the clergy supported wealthy elites and propagated social values that served their interests. Christianity developed in a communal climate that was rebellious against official Judaism, refusing its class-based ideology.

The scrolls (or manuscripts) discovered in the caves near the Dead Sea – unearthed in the second quarter of the twentieth century – revealed that the rebellious sect of the Essenes[5] had lived in isolation from the world. They organ-

---

3 Engels 1894–95.

4 Refers to the Indian social stratification system known as the caste system.

5 The Essenes were a Jewish religious sect (c. 2nd century BCE–1st century CE) known for their ascetic lifestyle, communal property, ritual purity practices, and apocalyptic beliefs, most famously associated with the Qumran community and the Dead Sea Scrolls. (A.K.)

ised themselves in monastic-like communities characterised by a form of collectivism that emphasised equality among members and strict adherence to spiritual virtues and ideals. Their worldview was shaped by a dualistic cosmology, in which an eternal struggle between the forces of darkness and the forces of light unfolded. The Essenes saw it as their duty to align themselves with the forces of light in order to hasten their inevitable triumph in the final reckoning.

Thus, the message of early Christianity appeared in the life of the first followers of Christianity, inspired by the 'Acts of the Apostles', who established a primitive socialist system where they pooled the resources of all members into one fund that met their needs (3).[6]

Given this context, it was natural for Christianity to attract the enslaved and the oppressed, leading to its spread among disadvantaged popular classes not only in the remote province of Palestine but also throughout the Empire, including in Rome, the heart of the Empire. However, Christianity soon began to transform,[7] and after a period of brutal persecution, it was eventually adopted by the ruling classes, becoming the official religion of the Roman Empire – both in the West, centred in Rome, and in the East, centred in Byzantium.

Marxist scholars contend that the wealthy ruling classes embraced Christianity for three reasons: first, it provided the underprivileged classes with the hope of happiness and justice in the afterlife; second, it offered the Roman Empire a unifying religion that could transcend social and ethnic differences; and third, it endorsed the class-based hierarchical system, as the advocates of Christianity, after its initial phase, did not oppose to the fundamental structures of class-based society.

Reliable information indicates that Christianity emerged during a period marked by escalating class conflicts between slaves and masters, and the weak-

---

6 Acts 4:32–35 (King James Version): 'And the multitude of them that believed were of one heart and of one soul: neither said any of them that ought of the things which he possessed was his own; but they had all things common ... Neither was there any among them that lacked: for as many as were possessors of lands or houses sold them, and brought the prices of the things that were sold, And laid them down at the apostles' feet: and distribution was made unto every man according as he had need'. Chapter 5 recounts that a man named Ananias and his wife Sapphira misappropriated the proceeds from the sale of their property and lied to the Apostle Peter when questioned. They were struck dead immediately, 'And great fear came upon all the church, and upon as many as heard these things'.

7 Many scholars believe that Paul the Apostle, who converted to Christianity later and was not one of the original apostles of Jesus, was the one who initiated the fundamental shift when he urged slaves to return to masters, citing a phrase attributed to Jesus: 'Render unto Caesar the things that are Caesar's, and unto God the things that are God's'.

ening of the sociopolitical Roman system. This period also saw the transition from slavery to feudalism, with Christianity gradually becoming a significant component in shaping national identity.

The temporal gap between the origins of Buddhism and Christianity is comparable to the gap between Christianity and Islam. Approximately six centuries after the advent of Christianity, Islam emerged in Mecca, located in the Hijaz, at the heart of the Arabian Peninsula – a region central to major economic activity.

For the purposes of this study, the extent of Jewish or Christian influence on Islam is not of primary concern. What matters is that Islam arose during a period when Mecca and the Hijaz were transitioning from a primitive communal system to a class-based one. Mecca was a cultural hub positioned between two major empirical blocs: India and Byzantium. Islam, with its emphasis on social justice, was embraced by the marginalised and oppressed social classes suffering under the harsh economic impacts of expansive trade. This trade, as contemporary chronicles describe in the context of summer and winter journeys, had led to the rise of a wealthy class that, rather than being content with its material wealth, began to monopolise public natural resources such as wells and meadows.

The Islamic call for social justice was reflected in the sociopolitical structure of early Islam during the Rashidun Caliphate. At this time, the concept of primitive socialism was evident in the *bayt al-mal* (House of Wealth), where all wealth from the Arab conquests was concentrated. This institution served as a public fund, pooling and equitably distributing resources among Muslim fighters.[8]

In this historical phase – following a harsh period of persecution and violent repression aimed at extinguishing the Islamic message – the dominant wealthy classes adopted Islam and began to wield it as a unifying banner in their efforts to consolidate the tribes and regions of the Arabian Peninsula, laying the groundwork for the establishment of an Islamic Arab Empire. This Empire expanded from the Arabian Peninsula to include surrounding Arab and

8 One of the companions of Prophet Muhammad, Abu Dharr al-Ghaffari, exemplified the notion of Islamic 'primitive socialism' when he rejected Muawiya's claims during the rule of the fourth Caliph, Uthman ibn Affan. Muawiya viewed the 'House of Wealth' as the state's treasury, while Abu Dharr insisted that it was the 'House of Muslims'. Through his opposition to the emerging class-based system accompanying the expanding Muslim Arab Empire, Abu Dharr publicly denounced the decline of Islam in mosques and markets, effectively announcing an uprising against it: 'And those who hoard gold and silver and spend it not in the way of Allah – give them tidings of a painful punishment'. (Quran 9: 34).

non-Arab regions, reaching as far as Andalusia (Spain) in the West and the borders of China in the East, while traversing North Africa.

Despite some similarities, Islam differed from Buddhism and Christianity not only in its temporal context but also ideologically. While Islam promised paradise in the afterlife to virtuous Muslims, it did not advocate withdrawal from worldly life or social isolation. Consequently, it did not foster monasticism as seen in Buddhism and Christianity, and Islamic monasteries did not proliferate within its regions.

This demonstrates that while Buddhism, Christianity, and Islam, as Engels suggested, accompanied significant sociopolitical changes, they were not the primary drivers of these changes. Rather, these sociopolitical transformations influenced religious doctrines. Initially, these religions emerged from a stance of resentment towards class-based sociopolitical structures that oppressed the poor and the marginalised. However, over time, they became tools of the elite who adopted and adapted these religions to reinforce and sustain class-based systems against their opponents.

Both Christianity and Islam exhibit a common phenomenon where revolutionary social movements sought refuge in religion and its doctrines. For these movements, religion served as an ideology that aided their struggles against rulers and authoritarian figures. In his examination of peasant revolts in rural areas and popular rebellions in European cities during the Middle Ages, Engels observed that these uprisings were often imbued with religious overtones. The peasants and common people were seen as striving to restore Christianity to its earlier uncorrupted state and to save it from degeneration. However, beneath this religious fervour lay materialist interests.

Throughout the era of the Arab Muslim Empire, leaders of social revolutionary movements leveraged Islamic doctrines, citing the Holy Quran, the Hadith (Islamic oral tradition), and the practices of the early Muslim Imams. Yet, as Engels observed, these movements ultimately aimed at effecting transformations in society's economic and political structures. It was anticipated that revolutionaries in the Arab Muslim Empire would draw on Islamic doctrines to shape their intellectual tools and social perceptions. Islam, unlike some other religions, did not separate the divine from the worldly nor advocate withdrawal from society. Instead, it established laws for sociopolitical conduct, blending the sacred with the secular. This integration was exemplified by the political system and the Caliphate, which combined spiritual and material authority.

In contrast, despite its spiritual mission, Christianity, once it established its institution and the Catholic Universal Church in Rome during the Middle Ages, attempted to unify the spiritual and temporal authorities. At that time, the popes led an unrelenting struggle and achieved some degree of success in certain feudal regions. Nevertheless, they ultimately failed to fully realise this unification and were obliged to accept a secondary role within the feudal ruling systems, focusing on maintaining control over the populace and supporting secular authority.

A parallel phenomenon can also be observed in the realm of secular authority within both the Christian and Islamic worlds during the medieval period – one that, in the Christian West, persisted up until the First World War. This was the claim that rulers governed by major religions, including Christianity and Islam, which continue to be followed by millions, have adapted to societal changes over time, thereby sustaining their influence. It was impossible for religion in a class-based society to change amidst shifting sociopolitical systems. This challenge was evident when Robespierre, a prominent leader of the French Revolution (1789), attempted to create a new religion based on social justice doctrines. His efforts failed as the emerging bourgeoisie showed little interest. After separating religion from the state and undermining the feudal and ecclesiastical resistance, the bourgeoisie later aligned with the clergy to counter the revolutionary forces. This alliance led to the formulation or practice of Christianity in ways that aligned with bourgeois interests. in such a project. Having already severed church from state and subdued the feudal lords and their clerical allies, the bourgeoisie was soon willing to reconcile with ecclesiastical institutions to suppress the growing revolutionary forces. In turn, these institutions reinterpreted Christian doctrine – or at least practiced Christianity – in a way that aligned with bourgeois interests.

CHAPTER 2

Social Ideologies in Islam

1 Pre-Islamic Mecca

The Arabian Peninsula has seen many kingdoms, some of which thrived in the south, such as in Yemen, while others were established in various regions of Iraq and the Levant, particularly along desert routes. It can be argued that the prosperity of these kingdoms and city-states was largely due to their involvement in trade, as they played a crucial role in facilitating cross-border commerce during that period. The transformations in trading patterns across the Arabian Peninsula were closely linked to changes in the fortunes of local Arab settlements. Amidst these dynamics, Mecca flourished and emerged as a prominent center in the sixth century CE.

In his book *Arab Markets In Pre Islamic* Era, Saʿid al-Afghani wrote:

> Over time, and along the route frequently traversed in antiquity, two major trading hubs emerged: Mecca and Madinah. These cities gained prominence, and their residents began trading with Yemeni tribes. By the sixth century CE, control of trade gradually shifted from the Yemenis to the Quraysh tribe of Mecca, whose status and power increased significantly, leading them to monopolize trade in the Arabian Peninsula, particularly during periods of security turbulence and hindered passage of Abyssinians and Nabataeans. Moreover, the primary factors behind the rise and prosperity of Meccan trade included the wars, conflicts, and competition between the Persians and the Romans.[1]

There is also evidence that Mecca has been a trade centre since ancient times. This status made it a house of gods and a sanctuary for pilgrims from neighbouring tribes, who also used it as a market to exchange goods and trade in various prevalent forms. However, this centre experienced a decline over time until it was revived in the fifth century. In his book *Bulugh al-Arab fi Maʿrifat Ahwal al-ʿArab*, al-Alusi notes that Quraysh established the system of the two major trading journeys[2] in the mid-fifth century, during a period when the village faced aridity and famine:

1 Al-Afghani 1960, pp. 20–1.
2 The Holy Quran states that: 'For the accustomed security of the Quraysh – Their accustomed security [in] the caravan of winter and summer – Let them worship the Lord of this House,

© 2027 KONINKLIJKE BRILL BV, LEIDEN | HTTPS://DOI.ORG/10.1163/9789004774261-007

> Hashim ibn ʿAbd Manaf organized the various clans of the Quraysh for seasonal trade expeditions – southward to Yemen in the winter and northward to the Levant in the summer. The profits from these journeys were distributed in a way that supported the poor, helping to establish a degree of economic parity between them and the wealthy. This arrangement remained in place until the advent of Islam.[3]

It may be inferred that Abraha the Abyssinian's campaign against Mecca – coinciding with the birth of the Prophet Muhammad in the Year of the Elephant – was aimed at reclaiming Yemen's former commercial standing, which had declined due to internal and external conflicts. By the sixth century CE, when Prophet Muhammad began his mission, Mecca's commercial development had reached a level that made it an 'international hub' during a period marked by the emergence of foreign trading houses.

In his book *Fajr al-Islam* (*Early Islam*), Ahmad Amin wrote about the shift of trade control from the Yemenites to the Meccans:

> Then, the Yemenites declined, and their place in the trade network was taken by the Arabs of the Hijaz starting in the sixth century. The Arabs of the Hijaz established Mecca as a center for their trading activities and protected the trade routes. On the eve of Islam, as hostility between the Persians and the Romans intensified, trade grew substantially. The Romans depended heavily on trade from the Hijaz, including luxury goods like silk. Some Frankish historians noted that in Mecca itself, there were Roman trading houses used by the Romans to conduct their commercial affairs and gather intelligence on the Arabs. Additionally, Abyssinians resided there to oversee their own commercial interests.[4]

In the context of commercial prosperity, it became evident that the class-based gap in society widened, with the wealthy becoming extremely affluent while the poor sank to the lowest levels of poverty and deprivation. This process of social polarisation, characteristic of all class-based societies, saw free poor individuals who could not repay their debts becoming slaves, thereby increasing the proportion of slaves as the wealth of major trading and affluent families grew. Furthermore, the system of large trading caravans, which comprised hundreds or even thousands of camels, required military manage-

---

Who has fed them, [saving them] from hunger and made them safe, [saving them] from fear' (Quraysh 106: 1–4).

3 Al-Alusi 1867–71, vol. 1, p. 368; cited in al-Afghani 1960, p. 35.

4 Amin 1964, p. 13.

ment and organisation. Scouts would precede the caravans, explorers would guide them along the routes, and guards would protect them. For the caravan owners, providing protection against the dangers posed by invading tribes was paramount, often achieved through methods such as intimidation and bribery.

The means of intimidation and bribery relied on the presence of fighters capable of withstanding attacks and safeguarding caravans until they reached their destinations. In this context, Bandali al-Jawzi wrote in his book *Tarikh al-Harakat al-Fikriyya fi al-Islam* (History of Intellectual Movements in Islam):

> This necessity compelled the caravan owners and the wealthy in Mecca to recruit numerous individuals to safeguard their goods and protect their caravans along the route. Predominantly, these guards were Abyssinians or African slaves, and their numbers increased progressively each year.[5]

This indicates that Meccan society was fundamentally based on trade and was divided into two primary classes: the merchant class, whose wealth varied, and the impoverished class, some of whom fell into slavery. Despite the annual increase in the number of slaves, as noted by Bandali al-Jawzi, their proportion remained relatively low. Consequently, Meccan society did not become a slave society to the extent observed in ancient Greek or Roman imperial societies. Furthermore, Mecca cannot be considered an isolated entity within the Hijaz; it maintained relationships with Madina and Taif, and some prominent Meccans owned land in Taif. In this context, and based on Al-Baladhuri, Saeed al-Afghani demonstrated that:

> The relationship between the people of Mecca and the inhabitants of Taif extended beyond usury and trade. The people of Mecca owned property in Taif, which they managed and utilized. For instance, Al-Abbas[6] owned land in Taif from which wine was produced and served to pilgrims. Additionally, the people of Quraysh held properties in Taif and traveled from Mecca to oversee them. Consequently, Taif effectively became an administrative extension of Mecca.[7]

Based on this and several other pieces of evidence, it is evident that landowners in Taif, who were originally from Mecca – a region not conducive to agricul-

5 Al-Jawzi 1928, p. 17.
6 Among the wealthiest figures in Mecca and the Prophet's uncle.
7 Al-Baladhuri, *Futuh al-Buldan*, cited in al-Afghani 1960, p. 62.

ture – were leasing their lands. These arrangements in the agricultural sector were known as *Mukhabara* which refers to the 'cultivation of land in exchange for a share of the agricultural yield, typically amounting to approximately one-third or another agreed-upon portion'.[8]

This suggests the existence of a class of landless farmers, as well as agricultural laborers working on large estates. Although detailed information about land ownership during this period is scarce, the descriptions of production and trade confirm that agriculture was practiced on a relatively large scale.[9]

Thus, the class structure of the Hijaz during that era – specifically in Mecca, Medina, and al-Ṭa'if – becomes clearer. Alongside the two essential classes, the merchants and the poor (since slaves did not form a distinct class or occupy a significant role in the economic structure), a third group emerges: the peasant-farmer class. Yet agriculture remained relatively limited, with trade holding a dominant position.

This economic reality is reflected in the Quran, which addresses trade extensively among its various topics, while referring to agriculture mainly in metaphoric terms – illustrating the sincerity or peril of faith. The dominance of commerce and the administrative system aligned with it has led more than one scholar to describe Mecca's governance structure at the time as a 'commercial republic'.[10]

In this discussion, we do not aim to extensively detail the features of what might be termed a 'republic', without overburdening the administrative framework of Mecca. Rather, we seek to highlight two main characteristics of the emerging sociopolitical thought of the period: first, the prioritisation and protection of the wealthy class, including measures so extensive that creditors could sell debtors into slavery; and second, the elevation of tribal solidarity (*'asabiyya*) as a principal foundation of social status and class position in society.

On the eve of the Islamic mission, this structure was further affirmed through the division of administrative responsibilities, including: the provisioning of water to pilgrims (*al-siqaya*), the offering of food and hospitality (*al-rifada*), the bearing of the battle standard (*al-raya*), the giving of counsel

8 Al-Afghani 1960, p. 51.

9 In his book *The History of the Jews of Arabia*, Israel Wolfson wrote that 'Trade was particularly among the most important aspects of life for the Jews in Hijaz, to the point that some gained significant and far-reaching reputations, such as Abi Rafi' Al-Khaybari … It could also be said that they were known for their trade in dates, barley, and wheat in Northern Hijaz. It is also evident that dates, barley, and wheat were produced in this region during that time. See Wolfenson 1927, p. 18.

10 The book of the orientalist H. Lammens *The Commercial Meccan Republic*.

(*al-mashura*), the arbitration of blood money and collective fines (*al-ashnaq*), the erection of the war tent (*al-qubba*) around which warriors would gather, diplomacy (*al-sifara*), and financial management – especially the collection of funds dedicated to the gods.

Rightly, Ahmad ʿAbbas Salih wrote in his book *al-Yamin wa-l-Yasar fi-l-Islam* (The Right and the Left in Islam): 'Authority in Mecca was exercised by a government composed of ten men who, in appearance, represented the various tribes, but in reality represented the commercial and financial power of the Meccan society'.[11] He illustrated this by naming those who held these posts, such as al-ʿAbbās ibn ʿAbd al-Muṭṭalib, who oversaw the siqāya; Abū Sufyān ibn Ḥarb, who directed matters of war; and Khālid ibn al-Walīd, responsible for the war tent, among others.

It was no coincidence then that the first three Caliphs of the Rashidun Caliphate were all merchants, two of whom were part of the Meccan government before the advent of Islam. Abu Bakr (11), one of the prominent merchants, was responsible for *al-ashnaq* (determining compensations and financial liabilities), while his companion, ʿUmar ibn al-Khattab (12) was responsible for *al-safara* (diplomacy) between Quraysh and other villages and tribes. These administrative posts were not only reflective of Mecca's mercantile structure but also foreshadowed the intense competition for power within the ten-man governing council that ruled Mecca before the advent of Islam. Historical sources preserve accounts of rivalries between two political alliances: the *Mutayyibun* – a coalition formed by the Banu ʿAbd Manaf, named after the ritual act of perfuming themselves when making their pact – and the *Ahlaf* – an alliance organised by the Banu ʿAbd al-Dar.

However, this struggle – essentially a rivalry between two branches of the noble Quraysh clan, both descended from Qusayy ibn Kilab,[12] the first to attain centralised authority in Mecca – persisted and later assumed new forms, driven by specific economic factors. Ahmad Abbas Saleh argues that this competition for power at the end of the pre-Islamic era was, in essence, a form of social conflict within the broader upper merchant class. He interprets the *Hilf al-Fudul*, an alliance formed by the clans of Banu Hashim, Banu ʿAbd al-Muttalib, Asad, Zuhra, and Taym, as a coalition of the less affluent commercial factions in contrast to the wealthier bloc led by Abu Sufyan.[13]

---

11 Salih 1972, p. 34.

12 Qusayy ibn Kilab, ancestor of the Prophet Muhammad, unified the Quraysh tribe and established their control over Mecca and the Kaʿba in the late 5th century CE, founding the system of tribal governance that dominated pre-Islamic Mecca. (A.K.)

13 Salih 1972, pp. 38–9; Abu Sufyan ibn Harb, (ca. 560–650 CE) leader of the Quraysh tribe

The Prophet Muhammad, whose familial and social affiliation lay with the *Ḥilf al-Fudul*, appeared at the outset of his mission to be reviving an older political struggle over power between the Hashimites and the Umayyads – a contest in which the Hashimites had historically lost and the Umayyads and their allies had prevailed.[14]

Even without relying on the *Hilf al-Fudul*, the reality remains that the Prophet's affiliation with a clan[15] considered among the lesser landowners in terms of wealth, and his call to limit the unchecked dominance of capital, drove Abū Sufyān – whose control over commerce had reached its peak – to perceive the Islamic message as a revolution against him. He thus fought it with all his might.[16] However, the internal tensions within the upper financial-commercial class and the social stratification among its factions were not the principal contradiction. The essential conflict was that between the wealthy and the impoverished – an antagonism that was reflected clearly in the Meccan *sūras*.

What is most significant is that the prevailing social thought was fundamentally class-based. It regarded wealth and the pursuit of its accumulation as the highest goal, while also considering tribal solidarity (*ʿasabiyya*) a necessary sociopolitical mechanism for organising relationships within Hijazi society. Naturally, the disparity in the social structure – between sedentary life in villages or towns and nomadic life in the desert – left a profound impact on social consciousness. This disparity prevented the transition from familial and tribal concepts to broader notions that transcended such divisions.

2 From Tribe to *Umma*[17]

The Islamic social thought, or the Islamic *Daʿwa* (Call to Islam), fundamentally challenged the prevailing norms of the pre-Islamic era known as *al-jahiliyya*. Without imposing contemporary classifications on Islamic thought, it can be

---

and father of the future Umayyad Caliph Muʿawiya, was Muhammad's primary opponent during the early Islamic period before converting to Islam at the conquest of Mecca in 630 CE. (A.K.)

14 Salih 1972, pp. 30–1.

15 Except for ʿAbbas, the Prophet's uncle, who firmly rejected Islam.

16 Salih 1972, 43.

17 *Umma*, often translated as "community" or "nation," represents A group of people united by shared historical bonds, which may include linguistic, religious, or economic elements, and who have common goals in belief, politics, or economics. (A.K.)

argued that the core message was to abandon tribalism in favour of unifying the tribes into a single nation (*umma*).

The Quran addresses this shift in perspective, as seen in the verse: 'O mankind, indeed We have created you from male and female and made you peoples and tribes that you may know one another' (Quran 49:13). It also emphasises that: 'The believers are but brothers, so make settlement between your brothers' (Quran 49:10) and 'hold firmly to the rope of Allah all together and do not become divided. And remember the favour of Allah upon you – when you were enemies and He brought your hearts together and you became, by His favour, brothers'. (Quran 3:103.)

Islam redefined interpersonal bonds by asserting that faith in God unites all people. The Quran even called for the abandonment of familial loyalty if it conflicted with faith: 'O believers! Do not take your parents and siblings as trusted allies if they choose disbelief over belief. And whoever of you does so, they are the ⌜true⌝ wrongdoers' (Quran 9:23).

In this context, the campaign against the nomadic Arabs or Bedouins was significant. These groups, embodying extreme tribalism, not only represented a challenge to social unity but also impeded civilisational development, which was beginning to take shape through urban settlement and organised society. Their attacks on caravans and incursions into settled areas were seen as obstacles to progress. The Quran reflects this view, describing the nomads as characterised by disbelief and hypocrisy: 'The nomadic Arabs ⌜around Medina⌝ are far worse in disbelief and hypocrisy, and less likely to know the laws revealed by Allah to His Messenger' (Quran 9:97). 'And among the Bedouin Arabs there are such as regard whatever they spend (in the Way of Allah) as a fine and wait for some misfortune to befall you' (Quran 9:98), However, the Quran also acknowledges the possibility of repentance among the nomads: 'However, among the nomadic Arabs are those who believe in Allah and the Last Day and consider what they donate as a means of coming closer to Allah' (Quran 9: 99).

Following the success of the Islamic mission, the subsequent era was marked by efforts to eradicate tribalism and ethnic divisions, aiming to unify people within an Islamic framework. This objective is underscored by the well-known *hadith*:[18] 'There is no superiority for an Arab over a non-Arab, nor for a Qurayshi over an Abyssinian, except in piety'.

The Prophet Muhammad consolidated this universal vision in his Farewell Sermon:

---

18 *Hadith*: the corpus of prophetic traditions that, together with the Quran, forms the foundation of Islamic jurisprudence (*fiqh*) and religious practice. (A.K.)

> O people, your Lord is one, and your father is one. All of you are from Adam, and Adam is from dust. The most honoured among you in God's sight is the most righteous. There is no superiority for an Arab over a non-Arab, or for a red-skinned person over a white-skinned person or vice versa, except in piety.[19]

This universalism, transcending ethnic and racial divisions, did not prevent some Arabs from interpreting certain Qur'anic verses as conferring upon them a particular distinction. Among such verses are: 'Indeed, We have sent it down as an Arabic Quran so that you may understand' (Quran 12:2); 'And so We have revealed it as an authority in Arabic' (Quran 13:37).

Other verses further elucidate why the Quran was revealed in Arabic, thereby granting the Prophet Muhammad's tribe a particular distinction.

This is elucidated in the verse: 'And thus We have revealed to you an Arabic Qur'an that you may warn the Mother of Cities and those around it …' (Quran 42:7). This concept is further clarified in the verse: 'And We did not send any messenger except [speaking] in the language of his people to state clearly for them …' (Quran 14:4) and 'And thus we have made you a just community that you will be witnesses over the people and the Messenger will be a witness over you' (Quran 2:143).

This notion was a driving force for the Egyptian 'Muslim Brotherhood', who advocated the idea of the Islamic bond as the defining principle in inter-communal relations, to uphold a special status for the Arabs and to revive the slogan: 'The dignity of the Arabs is the dignity of Islam, and the humiliation of the Arabs is the humiliation of Islam'.

3 Al-Shura (Consultative Council)

We posit that the philosophy of governance is secondary only to Islamic social thought. The essence of this philosophy is captured in the verse: 'O you who have believed, obey Allah and obey the Messenger and those in authority among you. …' (Quran 4:59). This principle is further elaborated in the verse 'And those who have responded to their lord and established prayer and whose affair is [determined by] consultation among themselves, and from what We have provided them, they spend' (Quran 42:38). The Holy Quran emphasises obedience to God as a perpetual duty, extending this call first to the Prophet and subsequently to those in authority. This framework, as evidenced through

19 *Musnad Ahmad* 23489.

various historical events, prevented the emergence of the idea that authority could be derived directly from divine grace or that rulers were representatives of God on earth in mainstream Islam. The lack of such arguments, which would suggest direct divine representation, underscores the significance of the principle of *shura* (consultation) in early Islam following the death of the Prophet Muhammad. Even after the end of the Rashidun Caliphate and the transition of power to the Umayyads and Abbasids – who transformed the caliphate into a hereditary institution – the caliphs could not substantiate claims of deriving their authority from God or being the Prophet's successors. Consequently, it became essential for them to be chosen through an oath of allegiance (Bayʿa) by those in authority, as all matters concerning the Muslim community required consultation. This distinction between divine and human authority, although a defining feature of Islam, naturally integrates spiritual, material, earthly, and religious aspects – an integration largely absent in Christianity. This separation was a major factor that facilitated the development of *ijtihad*.[20]

If we consider the broad democratic principle implied by the Qur'anic verse, 'conduct their affairs by mutual consultation' (Quran 42:38), along with the Qur'an's rejection of ethnic or tribal favouritism in favour of piety as the sole criterion of virtue, we can better understand the principle espoused by the Kharijites.[21] They held that the right to the caliphate belongs to any believer who, through the perfection of his piety and faith, becomes worthy of leadership – regardless of his lineage, and even if he were a Black slave – so long as the Muslim community freely chooses him.

While it may seem contradictory to argue that the caliphate did not claim to represent God or His Prophet, especially given that the term 'the Caliph of the Prophet' appeared in official records, this requires clarification. The official title of the caliphs was 'Commander of the Faithful' rather than 'Caliph of the Prophet'. The term 'Caliph' was used in administrative contexts, such as leadership and jurisprudence, but it did not extend to the prophetic realm, which remained a unique relationship between the Prophet and God.

Nevertheless, this did not preclude various interpretations, especially given that the Quran was not the sole source of *shariʿa* and legal rulings. Prophetic traditions, which encompass a comprehensive collection of the Prophet's daily interactions, sayings, and rulings, also served as a crucial reference point, establishing precedents for similar circumstances.

20 Independent legal reasoning (A.K.)

21 The Kharijites were a puritanical Islamic sect that emerged in the first civil war (*fitna*), rejecting both ʿAli and Muʿawiya's claims to the caliphate and insisting that leadership should be based solely on piety, not on tribal or family lineage. (A.K.)

On the issue of governance, the major division that followed the emergence of the Kharijite phenomenon was between Sunnis and Shiʿa. The Shiʿa maintained that the rightful claim to the caliphate belonged to the Prophet's family (*ahl al-bayt*), beginning with ʿAli ibn Abi Talib.

Despite these divisions, the mainstream Islamic perspective remained largely unchanged. It could be argued that the social thought reflected in the Quran, along with the practices prevalent at the dawn of Islam, rendered the governance system democratic. Although the first Caliphs were merchants from the Quraysh tribe, their prominence was due to their status and their role as the commercial elite. They embraced Islam, led its expansion, and established the state that followed the Prophet's mission.

4 Social Justice

It is evident that social thought in the Quran is embodied in addressing the socioeconomic structure and its decisiveness regarding relevant matters. We can, at this point, identify certain features that appear unequivocal and decisive, while others remain open to interpretation.

The most prominent and explicit of these features is the denunciation of the wealthy elite. This is clearly expressed in the verse: 'And those who hoard gold and silver and spend it not in the way of Allah – give them tidings of a painful punishment' (Quran 9:34) and 'Woe to every scorner and mocker who collects wealth and [continuously] counts it. He thinks that his wealth will make him immortal' (Quran 104:1–3), Lastly, but by no means least: 'May the hands of Abu Lahab be ruined, and ruined is he. His wealth will not avail him or that which he gained. He will [enter to] burn in a Fire of [blazing] flame. And his wife [as well] – the carrier of firewood. Around her neck is a rope of [twisted] fiber' (Quran 111:1–5).

Yet, this reproach towards the wealthy was not absolute or all-encompassing. It was primarily directed at those whose immersion in trade led them to neglect worship of God and, more critically, at the tyranny of prominent merchants and wealthy usurers who exploited the populace and subjected some to slavery. In light of this, the Quran is explicit on two points: it acknowledges class differences, as reflected in verses that address favouritism and urge caution against miserliness. 'And Allah has favoured some of you over others in provision' (Quran 16:71) and '... And let not those who [greedily] withhold what Allah has given them of His bounty ever think that it is better for them. Rather, it is worse for them. Their necks will be encircled by what they withheld on the Day of Resurrection' (Quran 3:180).

Second, and more significantly, is the Qur'anic call for social justice. This is articulated across numerous verses, perhaps most forcefully in those which critique mere outward religiosity while emphasising ethical and material obligations toward the marginalised. A striking example is: 'Righteousness is not that you turn your faces toward the east or the west, but [true] righteousness is [in] one who believes in Allah, the Last Day, the angels, the Book, and the prophets and gives wealth, in spite of love for it, to relatives, orphans, the needy, the traveler, those who ask [for help] …' (Quran 2:177).

The call to social justice [in the Quran] manifests in various forms. In some instances, it takes the shape of a stark warning about horrific suffering: 'No! But you do not honour the orphan, and you do not encourage one another to feed the poor. And you consume inheritance, devouring [it] altogether, and you love wealth with immense love. No! When the earth has been levelled – pounded and crushed – And your Lord has come and the angels, rank upon rank, and brought [within view], that Day, is Hell – that Day, man will remember, but what good to him will be the remembrance? He will say, "Oh, I wish I had sent ahead [some good] for my life." So, on that Day, none will punish [as severely] as His punishment' (Quran 89:17–25). In other instances, the call to social justice adopts a more flexible and peaceful tone: 'And whatever good you [believers] spend is for yourselves, and you do not spend except seeking the countenance of Allah. And whatever you spend of good – it will be fully repaid to you, and you will not be wronged' (Quran 2:272).

To achieve social justice, there was an urgent call to halt the collection of interest, which was depleting small merchants and consolidating wealth in the hands of prominent financiers and merchants. The Quran accurately describes usury as 'consuming people's wealth unjustly' (Quran 4:61) and rejected its equivalence to sale: 'Those who consume interest cannot stand [on the Day of Resurrection] except as one stands who is being beaten by Satan into insanity. That is because they say, "Trade is [just] like interest." But Allah has permitted trade and has forbidden interest' (Quran 2:275). The firm objection to usury is further reflected in the condemnation of usury agreements that existed prior to the Prophetic Mission (Quran 2:278).

It is no exaggeration to say that the call to charity and the pursuit of justice are prominently emphasised in the Quran, appearing in various verses as a divine command: 'Allah commands you to render trusts to whom they are due and when you judge between people to judge with justice' (Quran 4:58). The principle of social justice served as a central motive in the call to abolish slavery: 'And whoever kills a believer by mistake – then the freeing of a believing slave and a compensation payment presented to the deceased's family' (Quran 4:92); and 'but He will impose blame upon you for [breaking] what you intended of oaths. So its expiation is the feeding of ten needy people from the average of that which you feed your [own] families or clothing them or the freeing of a slave' (Quran 5:89). Furthermore, the Quran integrates the liberation of slaves into various aspects of human interactions to reinforce and promote this cause: 'Those who divorce their wives in this manner, then ⌜wish to⌝ retract what they said, must free a slave before they touch each other.' (Quran 58:3).

One could justifiably contend that the Quran's call for fair governance includes a strong emphasis on honesty, as reflected in the verse: 'O you who have believed, be persistently standing firm in justice, witnesses for Allah, even if it be against yourselves or parents and relatives. Whether one is rich or poor, Allah is more worthy of both. So follow not [personal] inclination, lest you not be just' (Quran 4:135).

Nevertheless, a just social system cannot thrive in a commercial or class-based society lacking the necessary moral foundations. For this reason, the Holy Quran advocates for truthfulness and integrity in all trade: 'And establish weight in justice and do not make deficient the balance' (Quran 55:9) and '… give full measure when you measure, and weigh with an even balance …' (Quran 17:35). The Quran sternly warns those who disregard this command: 'Woe to those who give less [than due], Who, when they take a measure from people, take in full. But if they give by measure or by weight to them, they cause loss' (Quran 83:35). These principles have evidently moved closer to legislation than mere social thought, but they are mentioned to illustrate the Quran's unwavering commitment to fostering social justice.

Legislation in the Quran also encompassed interpersonal relations and matters of inheritance, with the aim of establishing Meccan society on clearer and more equitable foundations. However, the social thought to which the Quran referred has been open to interpretation from the outset, as evidenced by the Quran itself: 'It is He who has sent down to you, [O Muhammad], the Book; in it are verses [that are] precise – they are the foundation of the Book – and others unspecific. As for those in whose hearts is deviation [from truth], they will follow that of it which is unspecific, seeking discord and seeking an interpretation [suitable to them]' (Quran 3:7). For this reason, Islamic social thought did not develop along a single trajectory, but rather along multiple, intersecting paths. This diversity of development was not primarily due to the intellectual capacities of the Companions or their successors, but rather to the social struggles that emerged in the formative period of Islam. These conflicts – and their social and ideological reverberations – constitute a series of ideological chapters that we may seek to explore in greater detail in subsequent sections.

CHAPTER 3

The Origins of Shiite Thought in Islam

Following the death of Prophet Muhammad, two interrelated processes unfolded – both naturally connected through their mutual interaction. The first was the establishment of the Arab Islamic State, which expanded significantly through major conquests. The second was the development of a sociopolitical ideology, which would both shape and be shaped by this new state. While the former process necessitated defining the nature of the supreme authority within the state, the latter relied on the interpretation of the Quran and the Prophet's Hadiths, which Muslims regarded as foundational intellectual pillars of Islam.

These two processes were inevitably influenced by the shifting dynamics of economic development and the evolving balance of class-related power, which continually changed in response to the circumstances of the conquests. The influx of wealth and resources into the central hub of the new state – Medina – and the increasing number of affluent Arabs across the Empire, along with their growing fortunes, also played a crucial role. The election of Abu Bakr Al-Siddiq (r. 632–34 CE) as the first caliph was neither premeditated nor based on established norms. Consequently, the method of his election did not set a constitutional precedent to which future authorities were bound, nor did it become a compulsory model for succession. Rather, it was a spontaneous decision, born of compromise, aimed at avoiding conflict among those competing for the Caliphate.

While most Arab historians, including all the prominent veterans among them, agreed that the conflict over the Caliphate following the Prophet's death was between *al-muhajirun* (immigrants) – those who accompanied the Prophet when he fled Mecca, thereby earning priority – and *al-ansar* (supporters), who welcomed the Prophet as a stranger in Medina and believed their claim to the Caliphate was unequivocal, several researchers have reconsidered this assessment. They approach the event through a materialist and objective lens, rather than an idealistic or simplistic one, concluding, as Ahmad Abbas Saleh did, that 'the choice of Abu Bakr al-Siddiq was entirely successful, for he was a man acceptable to both the right and left wings, and against whom the Ansar could not object'.[1]

1 Salih 1972, p. 58.

 | HTTPS://DOI.ORG/10.1163/9789004774261-008

Although the conflict was not explicitly apparent in the way we might expect today, it was evident from the outset in the differing opinions of the Prophet's companions, the narrators of his Hadiths, and the interpreters of the Quran – those to whom he entrusted its interpretation, fully aware of the dangers that misinterpretation could pose, and thus warning against it. In his book *Fajr al-Islam*, Ahmad Amin explained the reasons behind these differing interpretations, stating:

> The Prophet's companions were generally the most capable of understanding the Holy Quran because it was revealed in their language and they witnessed the circumstances in which it was revealed. However, they disagreed on interpretation due to differences in their interpretative tools. Their mastery of the Arabic language, though it was their mother tongue, varied. Moreover, while some were in the Prophet's constant company and directly witnessed the circumstances of a verse's revelation, others were not.[2]

However, this explanation remains subjective and does not penetrate to the root of the matter, for specific interpretations often arose from specific class positions. This truth became starkly evident during the exchange between the first Umayyad caliph, Muʿawiya, and Abu Dharr al-Ghifari – whom some writers affectionately call the 'first socialist in Islam' – concerning the public treasury (*Bayt al-Mal*).

Muʿawiya sought to define public wealth as belonging to God, arguing: 'Are we not the servants of God, and is not the wealth God's wealth?' In doing so, he aspired to legitimise his right to lead, positioning himself as God's representative on earth. However, Abu Dharr maintained that the wealth was:

> the wealth of the Muslims, the wealth gathered from the land belongs to the Muslims. You do not have the right to withhold any part of this wealth. You have defied the Prophet, Abu Bakr, and ʿUmar, keeping it for yourself and the Umayyads. Muʿawiya, you have enriched the rich and impoverished the poor.[3]

The importance of this debate lies in Abu Dharr's success – known for his piety and fear of God – in exposing Muʿawiya's deception. Muʿawiya, like the Umayyads of the time, followed Islam reluctantly. By invoking the concept of 'God's wealth', Muʿawiya sought to deny the people's rightful claim to it, feigning

2 Amin 1964, pp. 197–98.
3 Quoted in al-Khatib 1959, p. 252.

greater piety and obedience to God than Abu Dharr. His true position, however, became clear when, after expelling Abu Dharr, he delivered a sermon in the mosque, declaring: 'The wealth is ours, and the spoils of war are ours. We give to whomever we want, and deprive whomever we want'. In response, one of Abu Dharr's unprivileged companions retorted: 'The wealth is ours, and the spoils of war are ours. And whoever stands between us and these resources, we will bring him to judgment before God with our swords'. Abu Dharr deepened his class-based stance and call to resist the wealthy, citing the Quranic verse: 'And those who hoard gold and silver and spend it not in the way of Allah – give them tidings of a painful punishment' (Quran 9:34). He elaborated by saying: 'A Muslim is entitled to possess only what suffices for a day and night, unless the excess wealth is intended to be spent in the service of God'.[4]

Those who opposed this approach – without naming specific individuals but referring instead to the social stratum to which the rulers belonged – cited the verse: 'Do they distribute the mercy of your Lord? It is We who have apportioned among them their livelihood in the life of this world and have raised some of them above others in degrees [of rank] that they may make use of one another for service. But the mercy of your Lord is better than whatever they accumulate' (Quran 43:32).

Most crucial in this context is the conflict that erupted after the Prophet's death. In this struggle, Abu Bakr positioned himself in the political center, while 'Ali Ibn Abi Talib aligned with the left, provoking the resentment of the right wing, or the wealthiest men of Quraysh. He is the one who declared: 'No poor person starves except by the excesses of the rich' and 'I have never witnessed wealth in excess without seeing a rightful due left unfulfilled beside it'. When Abu Bakr chose 'Umar ibn al-Khattab (r. 634–644 CE) to succeed him as Commander of the Faithful, he selected a companion from his days in trade and an ideological comrade. Thus, one could conclude that 'Umar ibn al-Khaṭṭāb, the second in the Rashidun Caliphate, also belonged to the centrist faction.

Various authors woven legends around the religious strictness of 'Umar ibn al-Khaṭṭāb, his piety in practicing the faith, and his abundant administrative justice – so much so that he was given the title *al-Faruq* (the one who distinguishes between right and wrong). Yet, none of this altered the underlying trajectory of class development. This fact has been observed by more than one scholar. One such writer, Bandali al-Jawzi, states:

4 Al-Khatib 1959, p. 251.

> It is said that ʿUmar ibn al-Khaṭṭāb, known for his justice and severity, used to resist the tyranny of his governors, urge them to follow paths of justice, call upon them to show compassion toward their subjects, and threaten them with severe punishment if they failed in their duties. He would remove them from office and confiscate their wealth. However, these measures were not sufficient to prevent the leakage of public wealth – especially that belonging to the dhimmī population – into the pockets of officials, nor to stop the accumulation of wealth in the hands of certain individuals, which ultimately led to the emergence of a new affluent class in Medina, the capital of the new state.[5]

If we set aside the legendary accounts, we find that ʿUmar ibn Khattab was a product of his class, as evidenced by an event widely documented in historical accounts. During his tenure, Salman al-Farisi (the Persian)[6] served as governor of Kufa, earning a strong reputation, particularly for his support of manufacturers, their organisation, and the defense of their rights. This, however, angered the merchants and affluent individuals, who openly opposed him. Unable to overthrow him locally, they appealed to Caliph ʿUmar ibn al-Khattab, complaining about Salman's policies that negatively affected their business interests. In response, ʿUmar dismissed Salman immediately and did not appoint him to any position thereafter.

ʿUmar's class-based perspective became even more evident in the formation of the consultative council (*shura*) that he entrusted, before his death, with selecting his successor. The council was predominantly composed of the wealthiest individuals. More specifically, it consisted of seven men: ʿAbd al-Rahman ibn ʿAwf, one of the richest of the Prophet's companions; ʿUthman ibn Affan, a leading figure of the Umayyads and one of the wealthiest men; Saʿd ibn Abi Waqqas, a wealthy Qurayshite and a distinguished military leader in Islam; Ṭalḥa ibn ʿUbayd Allah and Al-Zubayr ibn al-ʿAwwam, both among the wealthiest companions; ʿAbd Allāh ibn ʿUmar, known for his asceticism and devotion, though excluded from the competition by ʿUmar; and finally, ʿAli Ibn Abi Talib. Given this composition, it was unlikely that the *shura* council, charged with selecting the third caliph, would choose ʿAli Ibn Abi Talib.

Thus, the selection of ʿUthman ibn ʿAffan was fundamentally a class-based decision. The exclusion of ʿAli, despite his military, civic, and religious qualifications, was similarly rooted in class interests. ʿAli, whom ʿUmar had frequently

5 Al-Jawzi 2015, p. 44

6 Salman al-Farisi (ca. 568–653 CE): a Persian companion of Prophet Muhammad, famous for suggesting the defensive trench strategy during the Battle of the Trench (627 CE) and representing the inclusion of non-Arabs in early Islam. (A.K.)

consulted in his final days, had by then become a rallying figure for those concerned with Islamic calls for social justice, drawing underprivileged and marginalised groups who saw in him a champion for their cause.

With the appointment of ʿUthman ibn ʿAffan, the contradiction between subjective inclinations and objective realities in governance began to fade. This dichotomy had been notably present during the reigns of Abu Bakr and ʿUmar, who had sought to achieve justice and equality, while simultaneously contending with the objective realities of an expanding Empire and increasing wealth. These dynamics, however, deepened class divisions, giving rise to a new tyrannical elite, whose interests were incompatible with the spread of social justice or alleviating the severe poverty of the labouring classes.

Under ʿUthman's rule, governance became a tool for the wealthy elite, aligning with their interests. Rather than curbing the accumulation of personal wealth, his policies encouraged its growth. A clear example of this can be seen in the policies of ʿUmar ibn al-Khattab regarding the Prophet's companions. Due to their social status, they were in the best position to capitalise on the expansion of the Arab Islamic Empire. ʿUmar restricted their movements to prevent them from acquiring land across the Empire, fearing that this would undermine the principles of social justice. He went even further by excluding land from the spoils of war, refusing to distribute it, and declaring it state property to be worked by labourers, who would pay land taxes and tribute in return.

However, ʿUthman abolished this restriction, allowing them to travel to other provinces, and begin purchasing palaces and accumulating resources. He extended this policy further, as he 'paid from the public treasury six hundred to Zubair ibn al-ʿAwwam, a member of the consultative council, and two hundred to another council member, Talha ibn ʿUbayd Allah, while also relinquishing part of a debt he owed him'.[7]

Within a short period, ʿUthman ibn ʿAffan initiated a profound transformation in the structure of governance. He dismissed the governors who had followed the path laid down by ʿUmar and replaced them with members of the Umayyad family – the same faction of wealthy elites that had opposed the Prophet during his lifetime. These new appointees acted in accordance with the interests of their class, which provoked widespread resentment among the general Muslim population and advocates of social justice, such as Abu Dharr al-Ghifari. Historical records recount that these advocates mobilised in opposition to ʿUthman's new regime, openly voicing their criticisms – clearly

7 Salih 1972, p. 79.

informed by class-conscious sentiments – and eventually moving from speech to action. Their resistance culminated in the well-known uprising, when delegations from various provinces arrived at the capital in Medina, ultimately deposing ʿUthman and bringing a definitive end to his rule by killing him in his own home.

The end of ʿUthman's caliphate marked a historic turning point – or more precisely, a crossroads – in the trajectory of the Arab-Islamic empire. At that moment, a fundamental question arose: in which direction would the nascent state now proceed? To answer this, it is essential to identify certain key dynamics that had begun to shape the internal structure of the emerging Islamic empire.

The expanding conquests beyond the narrow tribal borders of the Arabian Peninsula, reaching into the Persian and Byzantine Empires, had two major consequences: the influx of wealth on the one hand, and an accelerated process of intellectual exchange on the other. The flow of money, wealth, and slaves deepened social polarisation among the Arab tribes that had defended the Islamic faith. Additionally, the integration of Christians, Jews, Zoroastrians and Manichaeans[8] into Islam enriched Islamic thought with the social and spiritual ideologies of these religions.

Without diminishing the importance of the class-based politics pursued by ʿUthman and the Umayyads, it cannot be said that the immense wealth was accumulated suddenly during his caliphate, nor that the conflict began solely with his ascension to power. Rather, one could argue that quantitative changes led to fundamental transformations, culminating in heightened social contradictions that gave rise to multiple revolutionary upheavals over various historical stages. Furthermore, the conquest of vast provinces and the subjugation of peoples from the Persian and Byzantine Empires represented historical stages far beyond the tribal structures the Arabs had transcended. These conquests influenced the Arab-Islamic Empire in two critical realms: international relations and political systems.

The first effect was the escalation of national conflicts, especially as the subjugated masses, having lost their independence, realised that Islam's call for equality differed starkly from daily life practices. The second effect was the exploitation of the resources of these conquered peoples, whose development and social progress were accompanied by class struggle, which in turn sparked

8 Manichaeans: followers of Manichaeism, a dualistic religious system founded by the Persian prophet Mani (216–74 CE) that combined elements of Zoroastrianism, Christianity, and Buddhism, emphasising the cosmic struggle between light and darkness. (A.K.)

notable revolutionary movements. In light of this, some Arab scholars attribute the egalitarian positions of social equality advocates to the influence of Mazdakism.[9]

Ahmad Amin concludes that the 'socialism' of Abu Dharr was inspired by 'Abd Allah ibn Saba', a Jewish convert to Islam during 'Uthman's reign, who in turn derived it from Mazdakism. He writes, 'It is highly probable that Abd Allah ibn Saba adopted this idea from Iraqi or Yemeni Mazdakism, which was later embraced by Abu Dharr with good intentions, to which he added an ascetic dimension, as he was inclined towards it. For Abu Dharr was among the most pious and ascetic individuals'.[10]

Historians agree that Mazdak appeared in Persia during the fifth century CE, approximately two centuries before the era of the Rashidun Caliphate. He advocated for social equality. In his historical chronicle, al-Tabari wrote: 'Mazdak and his followers proclaimed that God provided humankind with abundant resources meant to be distributed equitably among them, but people have acted unjustly'. Al-Tabari further notes that Mazdak and his followers asserted their intention 'to take from the wealthy and give to the poor, from those who have much to those who have little'.[11]

One could reasonably point out a connection between Abu Dharr and the teachings of Mazdak, especially considering that some writers regard 'Abd Allah ibn Saba' as a possibly legendary figure, at least in this context. Nevertheless, the resemblance in their ideas is clear, and these similarities later became integrated into the ideology of early radical Shiites or their later successors. Thus, the period following 'Uthman's assassination brought together various factors that made the election of the next Caliph a pivotal moment in history. 'Ali ibn Abi Talib (r. 656–661 CE) was chosen as the fourth Caliph, but his status and the pledge of allegiance he garnered differed significantly from those of his three predecessors. During 'Uthman's reign, 'Ali had positioned himself as a leading figure in the opposition and acted as a mediator between 'Uthman and the rebels. As noted earlier, he attracted those who believed in the social equality promised in the Quran.

Moreover, 'Ali's pledge of allegiance followed an unprecedented social revolution in Islam, and as a result, it lacked the formal and broad consensus that

---

9 Mazdakism: a religious and social reform movement in 5th–6th century Sassanian Persia, founded by Mazdak, which advocated for the communal sharing of property and wealth, leading to significant social upheaval before its suppression. (A.K.)

10 Amin 1964, pp. 110–11.

11 Amin 1964, p. 109.

had characterised the pledges of the earlier Caliphs. Although the pledges to Abu Bakr and ʿUmar had stirred discontent among ʿAli's supporters, this division became more apparent during Ali's own election. This was reflected in ʿAbd al-Raḥmān ibn ʿAwf's refusal to pledge allegiance to Ali, a decision that Ali did not enforce. Additionally, Talha ibn ʿUbayd Allah and al-Zubayr ibn al-ʿAwwam withdrew their support, aligning with ʿAisha, the Prophet's wife, to revolt against him. They eventually allied with the Umayyad governor of Syria, Muʿawiya, enlisting him to wage war against Ali.

In light of this, ʿAli's election was seen as a victory for advocates of social equality and an effort to lay the foundations of a regime that would limit the influence of the wealthy on political authority. However, the subjective and objective conditions of the time did not allow for the creation of a system in which social classes would disappear. ʿAli ibn Abi Talib pursued a sociopolitical approach aimed at promoting equality within the limits of that historical period. He sought to implement Quranic teachings by interpreting them in a way that favored the poor over the rich. This is reflected in his advice and directives to his workers and the governors of various provinces. For instance, he instructed his tax collectors, saying: 'Be fair with the people and consider their needs; do not prevent them from fulfilling their necessities and requests'. Similarly, in his letter to his workers in Egypt, he wrote: 'Fear God in your treatment of the poor, the needy, the disadvantaged, and the afflicted … Take care of the orphans and the elderly, the helpless, and those who cannot seek aid themselves. This mission is burdensome for the governors, and being truthful is difficult'.[12]

Anwar al-Khatib rightly argues that the core principles of Caliph ʿAli's policies were rooted in what we now refer to as 'social welfare'. ʿAli assigned the state the responsibility of promoting development before collecting taxes, famously stating, 'Whoever demands taxes without fostering development ruins the land and destroys the people, and his stability will not last long'.[13]

Many commend ʿUmar ibn al-Khattab's statement, 'Since when did you enslave people, while they were born free?' However, it was ʿAli ibn Abi Talib who addressed all people, emphasising that they were born free, thereby offering a more profound understanding of freedom. George Jordac correctly distinguished between the two sayings, noting that 'the reader should not mistake the subtle difference between ʿUmar's words, which were directed at masters, instructing them not to enslave others, and ʿAli's words, which addressed

12 *Nahj al-balagha*, vol. 2.
13 Al-Khatib 1959, p. 234.

all people, telling them they were born free. This placed the matter of freedom in the hands of the people themselves, not in the hands of their masters, who could enslave or liberate them at will'.[14]

Historical developments led to the failure of Alī ibn Abī Ṭālib and the triumph of Muʿawiyah of the Umayyad dynasty. The transition from communalism (or primitive communism) to slavery, then feudalism, and later capitalism, shaped the conditions for the eventual rise of socialism. Among these conditions, the most significant was the affluent class – especially the commercial class at that time – which tipped the balance in favor of a classical class-based system, though with characteristics unique to the Islamic Arab Empire. Yet, historical developments and these objective laws ensured the continuation of the struggle for social equality.

Following the assassination of Ali, two key events unfolded on different levels: Muʿawiyah succeeded in establishing a hereditary caliphate, thereby ending the prior chaos associated with the election of the highest authority. This new system distanced itself from the original concept of the Caliphate and leadership of the faithful, leading Ibn Khaldun[15] to describe the period as the Umayyad monarchy rather than the Umayyad Caliphate.

The Shiite movement emerged, centered around Ali, who became a symbol of the aspiration for a better life. Over time, Shiism evolved into a vessel for rebellion – both spiritually and materially – against the prevailing system, whether Umayyad or Abbasid. It was, therefore, natural for Shiism to attract the oppressed, who faced persecution under the Arab Caliphate, with its deep-rooted tribalism, and who sought to struggle for a more just existence. In his book *Development of Muslim Theology, Jurisprudence, and Constitutional Theory*, D.B. MacDonald noted that Shiism has become an embodiment of social, religious, political, and economic protest, to the point where it was described as rejecting the advice and teachings of the Prophet Muhammad, retaining them only in appearance.[16]

The seeds of Shiism were sown following the Prophet's death and the emergence of the caliphate issue, though it may have begun during his lifetime. Al-Bukhari[17] recounts a conversation between al-ʿAbbas and Ali, indicating

14 Jordaq n.d., p. 110.

15 Ibn Khaldun (1332–1406 CE): North African historian and social scientist, author of the *Muqaddimah* (Introduction to History), widely regarded as a founder of modern historiography and sociology. (A.K.)

16 Macdonald 1903, p. 103.

17 Muḥammad ibn Isma'il al-Bukhari (810–70), renowned Islamic scholar and compiler of *Sahih al-Bukhari*, one of the most authoritative collections of Hadith in Sunni Islam. (A.K.)

that the Prophet's family (*ahl al-bayt*) believed the caliphate was their rightful claim. According to accounts, Al-ʿAbbas said to ʿAli, after realising the Prophet's passing was imminent: 'Let us go and ask him about this matter (the caliphate); if it is meant for us, we will know, and if it is for someone else, we will speak to him, so that he recommends us. ʿAli replied, "If we ask for it and he denies us this right, those who come after him will not grant it to us"'.[18]

Historians are largely in agreement regarding ʿAli's merit – his deep faith in Islam, his exceptional military prowess, his distinguished performance in battle, and the depth of his thought. They also affirm his fitness for the caliphate, noting that a significant number of Companions favored him over Abū Bakr, ʿUmar, and others. In this sense, a form of allegiance to ʿAli – *tashayyuʿ* – was known even during the era of the Rightly Guided Caliphs. Yet it is difficult to determine whether the majority of those who supported him at the time did so because he was a member of the Prophet's family and the husband of his daughter, or because of his personal qualities and suitability for leadership.

However, Shiʿism would grow into a religious-political movement, beginning its multifaceted and organisationally complex intellectual trajectory after Ali's assassination. It emerged amid a constitutional struggle that, though not always clearly delineated, was closely tied to questions of political authority. One can assert that the pledges of allegiance to Abu Bakr, ʿUmar, ʿUthman, and ʿAli were all conducted within the framework of a broad and loosely defined democratic vision – one grounded in the ideals of companionship with the Prophet, loyalty to Islam, and individual merit. It was within this context that the act of *bayʿa* (pledging allegiance) followed the process of selection. The practice of *bayʿa* thus came to embody the notion of *ijmaʿ al-umma* (the consensus of the community), as those who gave the pledge were seen as representing the will of the *umma*.

Regarding this practice, which helped unify supporters, immigrants, and the Prophet's companions from various tribes, two schools of thought emerged. One school held that the caliphate should belong to Quraysh, basing their argument on a Hadith of the Prophet, later cited by ʿAbd al-Qahir al-Baghdadi: 'The Imams are from Quraysh'. The second school asserted that the Imamate was the rightful claim of *ahl al-bayt*, particularly Ali, as ʿAbbas, the Prophet's uncle, converted to Islam after Ali.

However, following Ali's death, three distinct schools emerged. The first could be described as the pragmatic school, which argued that the constitutional issue had been settled with the rise of the Umayyads and the establish-

18 Amin 1964, pp. 266–7.

ment of their caliphate. This school later supported the Abbasids when they seized power from the Umayyads by force.

The second school, the Kharijites, split from ʿAli's party after the Battle of Siffin[19] and developed a democratic theory of the caliphate. They argued that the caliph should be chosen through the free will of the Muslim community, and once elected, he should neither renounce his position nor rule arbitrarily. The caliph need not be from the Quraysh tribe; he could belong to any tribe, even if he were an Abyssinian slave. Once elected, he would become the leader of the Muslims and must adhere fully to God's commands, or he would be dismissed.[20]

The Shiʿa school, whose doctrine gradually took shape, maintained that the caliphate was not vested in the Prophet's family (*ahl al-bayt*) in general – for otherwise the Abbasid claim to the caliphate would be valid – but specifically in Ali and his descendants.

These schools can be reduced to two if we address the issue of the caliphate within the religious framework and the positions of the two major Islamic groups: the Sunnites and the Shiites. The conflict between these two groups can be summarised in two points:

- The Sunnites believe that divine revelation ended with the Prophet, as the Quran and the Prophet's Sunna together form the complete message of God to humanity. In contrast, the Shiites believe that the message does not stop at a certain point, and that the Shiite Imams (hence why Ali and his successors are called Imams) complete the divine revelation to humanity.
- The Sunnites believe that the Prophet's caliphs are mortal, elected, and agreed upon by the *umma*, and that they may be elected from the Quraysh. The Shiites, however, believe that *ahl al-bayt*, especially Ali and his descendants, are the rightful Imams who continue the Prophet's message and fulfilling the revelation.

The differing approaches of Sunnis and Shiites expanded the scope of social and religious *ijtihad* – independent reasoning in the interpretation of Islamic

---

19 In this battle between the forces of ʿAli and Muʿawiya, the latter, on the brink of defeat, resorted to a ruse to avoid his loss. Muʿawiya's forces raised copies of the Quran on the tips of their spears, calling for arbitration based on God's book. Ali, recognising this manoeuvre as merely a war tactic, urged his forces to continue fighting. However, he was unable to convince the majority, and eventually submitted to call for arbitration. This decision provoked opposition from a group of fighters, primarily from the Banu Tamim tribe, who rebelled against Ali for accepting arbitration, questioning the sincerity of his leadership. They raised the banner of 'There is no ruler but God', thereby forming a radical faction within Islam.

20 Amin 1964, p. 258.

law – among Shiites, while it accelerated a process of ossification and rigidity among Sunnis. This reasoning carried within it a revolutionary potential that became central to the Shiite movement and ideology. As previously noted, the Shiite movement evolved into a broad current, representing a force that consistently rejected the prevailing systems of the Islamic Arab Empire across its various stages. It is important to note that this movement encompassed numerous tributaries.

One could argue that this current, which gained significant momentum, contained various factions, as the Shiites themselves splintered into groups. Some of these groups claimed the divinity of ʿAli and his right to be both a prophet and a messenger of God. Others asserted that the Prophet Muhammad had explicitly appointed ʿAli as his rightful successor and that the selection of the first three Caliphs was a violation of this command. In response to such claims, al-Shahrastani[21] remarked, 'If you claim that Muhammad chose his Caliph and that his Companions did not follow his orders, you thereby wrong the Companions of the Prophet'.

However, the core tenet of Shiite doctrine is the belief that Imam ʿAli was divinely appointed as the legitimate successor to Prophet Muhammad, and that the subsequent Imams should be his descendants, following the command of God. This includes the belief in ʿAli's divinity, evident purity, and infallibility, as he was never driven by self-interest or prone to spreading corruption or injustice within human society. Indeed, it is inconceivable, according to this doctrine, that God would choose any other Imam, for such a notion would imply that God is indifferent to the eradication of corruption.

It is not difficult to identify the reasons behind the spread of Shiʿa Islam, despite the terror, murder, and oppression it faced. ʿAli had become a legendary hero and an ideal symbol. His close relationship with the Prophet, his piety, and his vast knowledge made him, along with his successors, embody purity, religious integrity, and a revolutionary call to eradicate social and political injustices. The emergence of radical revolutionary branches, such as the Ismaʿilis within Shiʿa Islam, and their involvement in some of the most significant uprisings, such as the Qarmatian revolution, led supporters of the hegemonic regimes of the time – and their counterparts in modern times – to claim that Shiism had become a refuge for all those seeking to destroy Islam,

21 Abu al-Fath Muhammad al-Shahrastani (1086–1153 CE) – Persian Islamic theologian, philosopher, and historian of religions born in Shahrastan, Iran. Best known for his comprehensive work *Kitab al-Milal wa al-Nihal* (Book of Religious and Philosophical Sects), which systematically catalogued and analyzed various Islamic sects, philosophical schools, and other religious traditions including Christianity, Judaism, and ancient philosophies. (A.K.)

whether out of hostility or resentment, or those wanting to incorporate the teachings of their ancestors – Judaism, Christianity, Zoroastrianism, and Hinduism – or for those who sought the independence of their provinces and the detachment from the Empire'.[22]

However, facts demonstrate that Shiʿa Islam was, in its essence and general approach, a positive movement, and its branches represented revolutionary ideas and movements. It was further enhanced and consolidated due to the resilience of its continuous struggle and all the calamities it went through. And some scholars were probably right in their argument that the assassination of Hussein, the son of ʿAli, in the battle of Karbala[23] added to Shiʿa Islam the dimension of martyrdom, and a certain sacrifice (like the sacrifice of Jesus) leading to paradise.

Without going into detail, it can be stated that Shiʿism, in its broadest framework, is divided into two main branches. The **Zaydi Shiʿa** halted at the fifth Imam, Zayd ibn al-Hasan ibn ʿAli ibn al-Husayn ibn ʿAli ibn Abi Talib. Their teachings are close to those of Sunni Islam, and they do not believe that divine revelation (*wahy*) designates the Imamate. Rather, any *Fatimid* – that is, a descendant of ʿAli ibn Abi Talib and Fatima, the Prophet's daughter – who is learned, ascetic, courageous, and willing to rise up and fight for justice is eligible to be Imam.

The second branch is **Imami Shiʿism**, which includes several sects, most notably the **Twelvers** (*Ithna ʿAshariyya*), who recognise a line of twelve Imams; and the **Ismaʿilis**, who trace the Imamate through Ismaʿil, the son of Jaʿfar al-Sadiq. The latter group played a significant role in Islamic history and was known for its intellectual breadth. The Ismaʿilis saw the *Rasaʾil Ikhwan al-Safa* (Epistles of the Brethren of Purity) as part of their scientific and philosophical heritage. At one point, they advocated a revolutionary program that called for the abolition of large-scale land ownership and its free redistribution to the needy, as well as gender equality.

Without reaching a conclusive argument, one could observe that the primary division within Shiʿa Islam lies between those who believe that the disappearance of the last Imam is temporary, expecting his eventual return as the Mahdi (the spiritual leader), and those who either reject or downplay this theory. The difference is essentially between an idealism marked by detachment

22 Amin 1964, p. 276.

23 Karbala (680 CE) was the battle in which the third Imam, Husayn ibn Ali, the grandson of Prophet Muhammad, and his followers were killed by the Umayyad caliph Yazid I's forces, becoming a foundational event in Shiʿa Islam and has shaped Shiʿite history as a tragic history of the marginalised, who raise the banner of justice against the tyrants.

from reality and a future-oriented anticipation of salvation, versus a focus on materialism and the daily struggle within concrete conditions. It becomes evident, as is the case with Shiʿa Islam and other religions that await the return of the Mahdi (or the Messiah in Judaism, or the second coming of Jesus Christ in Christianity), that the longing for the Mahdi's return intensifies during difficult times, and diminishes when the opportunities and motivations for active struggle are more prevalent and compelling.

Considering this, Shiʿa Islam and its teachings occupy a significant status in Islamic social thought, representing a general current, but the role of some Shiʿa factions in enriching this thought, especially progressive thought, was greater, and we would return to this generalisation later where possible.

CHAPTER 4

The Revolutionary Faction within Ismaʿilism

In the chapter of his *Muqaddima* discussing Shiʿi doctrines on the Imamate, Ibn Khaldun explains that, according to the Shiʿa, the Imamate 'is not a matter of public concern to be left to the judgment or decision of the community. Rather, it constitutes a pillar of the faith and a foundation of Islam, which the Prophet could not overlook. He was therefore obliged to appoint an Imam, divinely safeguarded from all sin, whether major or minor'.[1]

This integrated conception of governance in Islam – uniting both temporal authority and religious leadership – has led many advocates of the more reductive notion of 'Islamic democracy', encapsulated in the Quranic phrase 'whose affair is [determined by] consultation among themselves …' (Quran 42:38), to regard the Shiʿi doctrine of the Imam's infallibility (*ʿisma*) as an essentially aristocratic model.

In his book *Duha al-Islam* (The Forenoon of Islam), Ahmad Amin shows a clear preference for Sunnism, arguing that within the framework of Islamic democracy, the emergence of concepts such as infallibility and the avoidance of error is highly improbable. He observes that the supporters of Shiʿa Islam, particularly toward the end of the Umayyad and Abbasid Caliphates, were deeply influenced by Persian traditions. He notes that 'many Persians were raised according to aristocratic royal traditions, inheriting from their ancestors a deeply-rooted respect to monarchy'.[2]

It is, therefore, unsurprising that Shiʿa Islam, which has persisted into the modern era in largely rigid forms, produced a Shiʿite aristocracy during various historical periods. This aristocracy established similar regimes in Egypt and other regions. Furthermore, given the conditions under which the Shiʿite movement emerged, it was unlikely to achieve organisational or intellectual unity.

1 Ibn Khaldūn n.d., pp. 352–3. The Arabic term rendered here as "divinely safeguarded" is *maʿṣūm*, a key theological concept in Shiʿi thought denoting the Imam's infallibility from both major (*kaba'ir*) and minor (*sagha'ir*) sins (A.K.).

2 Amin n.d., p. 272. Amin's argument has been contested by numerous modern Shiʿi scholars, including Muhammad Baqir al-Sadr and Sayyid Muhsin al-Amin, who reject the reduction of Shiʿism to a mere continuation of Persian political culture. They argue that *ʿisma* is a Qur'anic and prophetic concept rooted in Islamic revelation rather than in pre-Islamic monarchic tradition. For a detailed refutation, see al-Ṣadr 1984, pp. 45–58; al-Amin 1983, pp. 118–24 (A.K.).

 | HTTPS://DOI.ORG/10.1163/9789004774261-009

With its popular roots and the association of its leadership with social justice, particularly in the context of the conflict between ʿAli ibn Abi Talib, the symbolic figure of Shiʿa Islam, and Muʿawiya, the governor of Syria and the first Umayyad caliph, the Shiʿite movement became a vessel for social rebellion and national conflict.

The vast Shiʿite movement inevitably encompassed diverse approaches due to ongoing shifts in the balance of class forces within Arab Islamic society, the concrete relationships between the Arab people and other nations, and the nature of the social forces that rallied around the Imams. The Shiʿite mission was also shaped by the specific conditions prevalent in each region. These differences were reflected in the numerous Shiʿa factions and their secondary branches, many of which disappeared when their leaders did.

One cannot overlook the subjective factor and the loyalty that was at times decisive in the emergence of certain factions. Moreover, the pressure exerted by the prevailing authorities – whether Umayyad or Abbasid, central or regional – largely shaped the direction and objectives of one faction or another. In this context, the violence stemming from persecution and the severe restrictions imposed on the Shiʿa not only explain the emergence of '*Mahdism*' but also the practices of '*taqiyya*' (precautionary dissimulation) and '*batiniyya*' (esotericism). Faced with these oppressive conditions, Shiʿa advocates proclaimed the coming of the *Mahdi*, who would bring justice to a world filled with tyranny and injustice. Additionally, they urged the continuation of their mission despite brutal repression, turning to *taqiyya* and esotericism as survival strategies. *Taqiyya*, in particular, involved self-preservation through discretion, outwardly displaying what one did not inwardly believe. In contemporary terms, this can be understood as the underground activism of revolutionary movements when terrorism escalates, and the ruling authorities obstruct the path to public action.

It is certain that the tragic fate of many Imams and their advocates played a decisive role in shaping the esoteric path within Shiʿa thought, which was later integrated into an intellectual framework that combined various philosophical approaches. It is well-known that most of the Twelve Imams, who together form the central figures of Shiʿite leadership, met violent or unnatural deaths. For instance, ʿAli ibn Abi Talib was assassinated, his son Hasan was allegedly poisoned according to Shiʿa sources, and his brother Husayn was killed in an unequal battle against the army sent by Muʿawiya's successor, Yazid. Moreover, Jaʿfar al-Sadiq, Musa al-Kadhim, ʿAli al-Ridha, and Muhammad al-Jawad were all believed to have been poisoned, and many Shiʿa advocates were killed during the Shiʿa revolts and uprisings throughout this period.

Taqiyya became intertwined with the concept of the Hidden Imam,[3] and subsequently, it became a core component of Shiʿa religious thought. This was reflected in a dual intellectual-philosophical approach, where everything was believed to possess both a hidden and a visible side, with two faces to every truth. This opened the door to liberal thought and critical inquiry. The rational approach, combined with the secretive organisational structure and the preservation of principles within increasingly restrictive frameworks as a Shiʿa individual ascended in rank, provided an opportunity for opponents of Shiʿa Islam to distort or misinterpret its beliefs. In the best case, they simply overburdened these beliefs with misrepresentation.

Al-Shahrastani explained esotericism as follows: 'The ancient *batiniya* (esotericists) mixed their discourse with some of the philosophers' teachings and compiled their books according to this methodology. They said concerning the Divine Being (*al-bari*), exalted be He: 'We do not say that He is existent nor non-existent, nor knowing nor ignorant, nor capable nor incapable', and likewise regarding all attributes. For true affirmation necessitates a partnership between 'Him' and all other existents in the aspect which we have attributed to 'Him', and that constitutes anthropomorphism (*tashbih*). Therefore, neither absolute affirmation nor absolute negation can be validly applied'.[4]

As for al-Ghazali,[5] in his treatise refuting the *batiniyya*, he determined: 'In sum, it is a doctrine whose outward appearance is Shiʿite rejection (*rafd*) while its inner reality is pure disbelief (*kufr*), and its key principle is the restriction of all sources of knowledge to the pronouncements of the infallible Imam, while dismissing reason from being capable of apprehending truth due to the doubts that afflict it'.[6] Given this complexity, it is sometimes difficult to trace the developments and historical trajectory of Shiʿa Islam, particularly because Shiʿa figures themselves, through the use of discretion and secrecy, at times enabled the distortion of their positions. Nevertheless, one must distinguish between the mainstream Shiʿa tradition with its common features and the various branches, each of which has its own distinct principles.

---

3 The Hidden Imam refers to Muhammad al-Mahdi ibn Hassan al-ʿAskari, the twelfth Imam in Twelver Shiʿa Islam, believed to have gone into occultation (*ghayba*) in 874 CE and expected to return as the Mahdi to establish justice on earth before the Day of Judgment.

4 Cited in Ghannan 1959, p. 283.

5 Abu Hamid al-Ghazali (1058–1111 CE) was an Islamic theologian, philosopher, and mystic, known as 'Hujjat al-Islam' (Proof of Islam), whose works like *The Revival of the Religious Sciences* and *The Incoherence of the Philosophers* profoundly influenced Islamic thought by integrating Sufism with orthodox theology.

6 Amin 1933, p. 284.

1 The Context of the Isma'ilism's Emergence

Sayyid Amir Ali wrote in his book *A Short History of the Arabs and Islamic Civilization* regarding the circumstances of Isma'ili origins:

> In the year 148 AH / 765 CE, the Imam Ja'far al-Sadiq (the sixth Imam) died in Medina. However, the scholarly circle, fortunately, did not cease with his death, as it continued to flourish under the leadership of his son and successor Musa, known as 'al-Kazim'. From that time began the division among the Shi'ites concerning the office of the Imamate, since Imam Ja'far had designated his son Isma'il, who died during his father's lifetime, so Ja'far made a second designation to his son Musa. However, some Shi'ites refused to recognize him and affirmed the Imamate of Habib ibn Isma'il. This disagreement marked the beginning of the emergence of the Isma'ili sect, which established the Fatimid State.[7]

Historians agree on the conditions and motives that led Imam Ja'far al-Sadiq to designate his son Musa as his successor instead of Isma'il. Scholars argue that Imam Ja'far 'refused to appoint his son Isma'il as his successor and the next Imam due to his behavior and reputation, as he was reportedly addicted to alcohol'.[8]

Others believe that Imam Ja'far appointed Musa as the future Imam following the death of Isma'il during his father's lifetime. They assert that the division among the leading Shi'a resulted from certain Shi'ite factions rejecting Musa's designation as Imam after Isma'il, viewing it as a violation of the 'Imam's infallibility' and the right of his descendants to inherit the Imamate. To support this claim, they attributed prophetic abilities and miracles to Isma'il, believing either that he was resurrected after his death or that he did not die, but rather disappeared and would reappear when the appointed time comes.

In his book *Zahr Al-Ma'ani* (The Flower of Meanings), the Isma'ili preacher wrote that 'Isma'il died, was buried, and reappeared alive in Basra, where people flocked to him, claiming that Isma'il ibn Ja'far had returned to life. He then placed his hand on the back of an elderly sick man and healed him'[9] (*al-Hakim bi-Amr Allah*). The Isma'ilis are referred to as 'Sab'iyya' because they belong to the Shi'ite faction that stopped at the seventh Imam, Isma'il, considering him the Mahdi. However, this label is not entirely accurate, as several

7 Ali n.d., p. 194.

8 Al-Jawzi 1928, p. 103.

9 'Imad al-Din Idris, *Zahr al-Ma'ani*, cited in Ghannan 1959.

Imams succeeded Ismaʿil, culminating in the emergence of ʿUbayd Allah al-Mahdi.[10] This period is known as the Era of the Hidden Imams, during which they adhered to 'secrecy and concealment to evade persecution and threats to their lives, until the time came for them to appear publicly'.[11]

Here, the question arises: under what circumstances did Ismaʿilism emerge? In 136 AH / 754 CE, the caliphate of Abu al-ʿAbbas ʿAbd Allah al-Saffah, the founder of the Abbasid state, came to an end, and the caliphate passed to his brother Abu Jaʿfar al-Mansur. This was during the time of the sixth Shiʿite Imam, Jaʿfar al-Sadiq, renowned for his philosophical reflections. Some believe that Wasil ibn ʿAta', the founder of the Muʿtazila school, was among his disciples.

It was during this period that Ismaʿil appeared, and his activity seemed to extend beyond scholarship and philosophy, as he led a tumultuous life, contributing to the rumors surrounding his notoriety. More significantly, the transition from the Umayyad to the Abbasid Caliphate was not merely a transfer of power but rather an 'ideological triumph'. The Abbasids, through their struggle against the Umayyads, asserted their claim to the caliphate. They regarded the Shiʿites as allies in their rejection of the Umayyads' claim to the caliphate, though the Shiʿites did not recognise the Abbasids' claims. The conflict between the Umayyads and Abbasids brought the issue of the caliphate and other religious questions to the forefront of debates within Arab-Islamic society, especially in the eastern provinces of the Empire. This environment enabled the Shiʿites to spread their ideas and invite people to embrace their principles. However, once the Abbasids defeated the Umayyads, they persecuted the Shiʿites even more harshly than their predecessors. Ahmad Amin suggested that the 'Abbasids' heightened severity towards the Shiʿites stemmed from their deeper understanding of Shiʿite inner workings, having closely interacted with them during the Umayyad period'.[12]

The persecution reached its peak during the caliphate of al-Mansur, from 136 AH / 754 CE to 158 AH / 775 CE. This era was marked by the consolidation of Abbasid authority, the enhancement of the caliph's prestige, and his glorification. Some historians attribute al-Mansur's hostility towards the Shiʿites to an event that occurred before the establishment of the Abbasid Caliphate. At that time, the prominent figures of *ahl al-bayt* gathered to discuss the

10 ʿUbayd Allah al-Mahdi (873–934 CE) was the founder and first caliph of the Fatimid dynasty, who established Fatimid rule in North Africa in 909 CE, claiming descent from Fatima (daughter of Prophet Muhammad) and Ali, and initiating the Ismaʿili Shia caliphate that would later conquer Egypt.

11 Ibid.

12 Amin 1964, p. 275.

decline of the Umayyad Caliphate and to plan a takeover of power. During this pivotal meeting, which al-Mansur attended, all those present – including al-Mansur himself – pledged allegiance to Muhammad, the grandson of al-Hasan ibn Ali, the second Imam, also known as 'Al-Nafs Al-Zakiyya' (The Pure Soul).[13] According to this account, al-Mansur's fear of Muhammad and the other Shiʿites was evident, leading him to persecute and attempt to eliminate them.

It is difficult to determine whether the spark that ignited the conflict between the Abbasids and the Shiʿites was al-Mansur's persecution or the Shiʿite leaders' disillusionment with the outcome of the struggle against the Umayyads. The sense that the Abbasids had seized the caliphate by force – an opportunity the Shiʿites felt they had missed for a second time – likely fueled their rebellion, not only during al-Mansur's rule but throughout the Abbasid period. What is certain is that Muhammad and his brother Ibrahim continuously resisted al-Mansur, and their forces were on the verge of victory. However, the Abbasid caliph ultimately defeated and killed them in 145 AH.

The death of Muhammad 'Al-Nafs Al-Zakiyya' and his brother Ibrahim marked the beginning of a brutal campaign that claimed the lives of many nobles of Basra. Al-Mansur ordered the execution of all Shiʿite supporters, the destruction of their homes, and the devastation of their orchards. He also confiscated the property of the descendants of al-Hasan and al-Husayn, revoked all their privileges, and threatened Imam Jaʿfar al-Sadiq. This violent campaign of terror and persecution during al-Mansur's reign created the conditions for the emergence of *taqiyya* (dissimulation) and esotericism, closely associated with Ismaʿilism and the insistence on Ismaʿil's Imamate. Ismaʿil lived during this period and died in 143 AH / 760 CE.

2 Ismaʿili Social Ideas

It is challenging to present a clear picture of the social ideas associated with early Ismaʿilism, as Imam Ismaʿil died young, and his historical biography is somewhat obscured. Some scholars have suggested that ʿAbdallah ibn Maymun[14] was the true founder of the Ismaʿili school or that he played a key role in

13 Al-Jawzi 1928, p. 190.

14 ʿAbdallah ibn Maymun al-Qaddah (d. c. 874–75 CE) was a key figure in early Ismaili Shia organisation and propaganda, considered by some sources as the architect of the revolutionary movement that led to the establishment of the Fatimid caliphate, though his exact role remains debated among historians.

developing and solidifying its foundational principles. Others argue that Ibn Maymun is merely a legendary figure, with no historical basis. Most significantly, opponents of Shiʿa, accused Ibn Maymun of atheism, claiming he was influenced by Greek philosophy.

The orientalist Reinhart Dozy supported this view in his examination of Ibn Maymun's principles. He wrote that Ibn Maymun aimed 'to integrate both the conqueror and the conquered into a single entity, forming a united community whose members are ranked hierarchically – from liberal intellectuals, who view religion as a tool for subjugating the masses, to extremists from all factions. He sought to turn believers into mindless instruments that empower skeptics and to push victors to deconstruct or alter the very state they had established'.[15]

While the process through which Ismaʿili ideas evolved in the social realm remains unclear, it can be confirmed that these ideas drew from a rational philosophical outlook and political experiences, which led the Ismaʿilis towards clandestine activism. Without delving deeply into their philosophical views, it is clear that the Ismaʿilis held a strong belief in the supremacy of reason and its capacity to comprehend the universe. They also valued dialectical reasoning as a method of arriving at the truth. Al-Shahrastani, in his attempt to explain this perspective, wrote:

> It was said in ancient times that God is neither eternal nor created. What is eternal are His commands and words, while what is created is the material world He fashioned. First, He created the Intellect, mighty and complete, and through it, He created the Soul, which is incomplete. For the Soul to attain the perfection of the Intellect, it must move from a state of imperfection to one of perfection. And to achieve this, the Soul requires a tool to propel it forward.[16]

The Ismaʿilis believed that true religion lies in humanity's ability to ascend, through perseverance and gradual advancement, to an understanding of the stages the universe has traversed since it separated from God – referred to as 'the Absolute Intellect'.[17]

This belief reflects the Ismaʿili adherence, like other Shiʿa factions, to the concept of the Imam's infallibility and absolute authority, as the Imam is regarded as the embodiment of the Universal Intellect. At the same time, this philosophical and dialectical framework, rooted in a deep trust in reason, paved

15 Reinhart Dozy, cited in Ghannan 1959, p. 285.
16 Ghannan 1959, p. 282.
17 Al-Jawzi 1928, p. 106.

the way for progressive social conclusions, particularly as class struggles intensified in Arab Islamic societies. Consequently, Ismaʿilism was able to embrace the principle of gender equality.[18]

However, one must approach the study of Ismaʿilism with caution, as the movement expanded and came to encompass various currents and factions, each with its own differences and nuances. For instance, the Druze, who emerged from Ismaʿilism and trace their origins back to the Fatimids as an Ismaʿili offshoot, do not adhere to the principle of gender equality.

There was a significant disparity in the thoughts and conduct between the Fatimids and the Qarmatians, an Ismaʿili faction that ruled in al-Hasa.[19] Over time, their reign expanded to encompass vast regions of Iraq and the Arabian Peninsula. These social ideas were shaped by the specific conditions and contexts of the regions they governed, as well as the stage of social conflict prevalent in each area. Bandali al-Jawzi succinctly summarised the ideas of the revolutionary Ismaʿili current, noting that they advocated for resistance against ethnic chauvinism and promoted a genuine fraternity, not only among Muslims but across all people, regardless of ethnicity, class, or religion. This fraternity was not based on religious unity, as was customary in both Islam and Christendom during the Middle Ages, but rather on the imperatives of sound intellect.[20]

In the economic realm, they called for the abolition of private land ownership and the redistribution of land to the needy. In his *Safar-nama*, the 11th-century traveler Nasir-i Khusraw described what he witnessed in Al-Hasa. He noted that the people claimed descent from Abu Saʿid,[21] who had promised to return after his death. Before his passing, he entrusted his six sons to govern with justice, aided by six ministers who collectively made decisions on all matters. Khusraw further observed that at the time, there were 30,000 Black and Abyssinian slaves engaged in agriculture and horticulture. The Qarmatians did not collect tithes from their subjects, and if anyone fell into poverty or debt, the state would support them until they were able to resolve their difficulties. Moreover, if one person owed a debt to another, they were not permitted to

18 Al-Jawzi 1928, p. 109.

19 Al-Hasa (also al-Ahsa) is an oasis region in eastern Arabia that historically served as a center of Ismaʿili Qarmatian power from the late 9th to 11th centuries, where the Qarmatians established a revolutionary state based on egalitarian principles before being absorbed into other Islamic polities.

20 Al-Jawzi 1928, p. 109.

21 Here Tuma is referring to Abu Saʿid al-Jannabi (d. 913 CE) who was the founder of the Qarmatian state in Bahrain and al-Hasa, who established a revolutionary Ismaʿili republic based on communal ownership and egalitarian principles, and whose followers later sacked Mecca and seized the Black Stone in 930 CE.

demand more than the original sum. If a stranger arrived in the city seeking to work, they were provided with the necessary funds to acquire all materials and tools, which were to be repaid to the state whenever possible. Al-Ḥasā also had mills owned by the Sultan, where grain was ground free of charge for the public, with the Sultan covering the wages and maintenance costs of the millers.[22]

It is important to pause here and examine the contradiction inherent in this supposedly just regime, which nonetheless maintained 30,000 Black and Abyssinian slaves. Although Nasir Khusraw visited Al-Hasa towards the end of the Qarmatian era, one might infer that these 'slaves' were not slaves in the conventional sense, but rather state-employed laborers working on farms and in orchards. This leads us to a broader examination of Ismaʿili social ideas as represented by one of its revolutionary branches, the Qarmatians, and to underscore that these ideas were shaped by the stage of development in the forces and relations of production.

This raises the following question: What was the relationship between this revolutionary Ismaʿili current and similar movements that emerged in the Persian provinces? Mazdak, who appeared two centuries before Islam, was the first known preacher for equality in the region, arguing that people are born equal and should live equally. He maintained that God had provided sustenance on Earth to be shared equitably among all people. However, human injustice led to inequitable distribution and widespread oppression.

It is evident that Mazdakite ideas remained deeply ingrained in the Persian cultural landscape, particularly in impoverished regions such as Azerbaijan, long after the demise of Mazdak and the suppression of Mazdakism. Given this, it becomes clear that Ismaʿilism and its clandestine movement, which naturally garnered support from the poor, the rebellious, and those discontented with the ruling authorities, were influenced by these social ideas. Moreover, the revolutionary Ismaʿilis lent their support to Babak al-Khurrami (d. 838 CE),[23] who emerged in Azerbaijan and confronted the Abbasid Caliphate in the 9th century CE (3rd century AH). Babak's call for land redistribution continued the legacy of Mazdak, reflecting the desperate need of impoverished peasants for land. Bandali al-Jawzi affirmed the existence of this connection, remarking that Mazdak's teachings continued to resonate among the people of Azerbaijan and its surrounding areas, attracting disaffected groups such as Persians, radical

22 Khusraw 1970, p. 143.

23 Babak al-Khurrami (d. 838 CE) was a Persian revolutionary leader who led a major revolt against the Abbasid Caliphate from 816–37 CE in Azerbaijan and northwestern Iran, drawing on Khurramite religious beliefs and social revolutionary ideals before being defeated and executed by the caliph al-Mu'tasim.

Shiʿites, and esotericists. This set the grounds for Babak's broader movement and paved the way for revolutionary movements within Islam to adopt Shiʿa ideology, telling the story of one of the greatest struggles for a better life and the right to Caliphate, as they claimed descent from *ahl al-bayt*.

CHAPTER 5

Muʿtazila – The Rationalist Ideology

The battle between the fourth Caliph, Ali ibn Abi Talib, and Muʿawiyah ibn Abi Sufyan – driven by envy over the Caliphate – was decisive both politically and intellectually. It marked the transition from the republic (as the Rashidun Caliphate is often referred to) to monarchy (the hereditary Umayyad Caliphate) in the political sphere. Intellectually, it contributed to the rise of various movements, such as the Kharijites, the Shiʿa, and the Murji'a.[1] This period also significantly impacted the Muʿtazila, the most influential political-philosophical school of thought during the era of the Arab Islamic Empire.

1 Intellectual Background

As the Umayyad Caliphate stabilised (40–142 AH / 661–750 CE), Muslim scholars began to explore their religion's deeper matters for various reasons. Chief among them were the urgent need to address emerging socio-political issues and the expansion of the Islamic Arab Empire, which brought with it increasingly complex challenges. Additionally, scholars faced the necessity of confronting the ideologies of other religions.

Over time, as intellectual exchange with rich traditions such as Indian and Greek philosophy intensified, Muslim thinkers were influenced by the achievements of other cultures, enriching their own intellectual frameworks. The first major controversy revolved around the issue of human free will: man's ability to choose between good and evil, juxtaposed against the concept of destiny pre-

1 A faction originally composed of some of the Prophet's Companions who refrained from involvement in the conflict among Muslims during the final days of Uthman, later evolved into a political movement following the eruption of the conflict between ʿAli and Muʿawiya. This political movement further developed into a theological current that explored the definitions of 'faith', 'disbelief', and 'believer'.

The core of Murji'ah thought rested on their rejection of the partisan bias exhibited by the Kharijites, the Shiʿa, and the Umayyads, who accused opposing leaders of deviating from true Islamic teachings. Murji'ah advocates maintained that all such judgments should be left to God, who would ultimately decide whether Uthman had committed blasphemy or if ʿAli had done wrong. Their theological approach evolved into a religious school whose main tenet was the sufficiency of belief in God and His prophets, without an emphasis on religious duties. In this regard, they demonstrated remarkable tolerance.

 | HTTPS://DOI.ORG/10.1163/9789004774261-010

determined by God. This gave rise to the *qadariyya* in 50 AH / 671 CE, a school that asserted that man is free in his actions and capable of creating his own deeds, independent of divine will.[2]

The leaders of the qadariyya, proponents of the freedom of choice, found ample support in the Quran, citing verses such as: 'Indeed, we guided him to the way, be he grateful or be he ungrateful' (Quran 76:3); 'And, [moreover], this is My path, which is straight, so follow it; and do not follow [other] ways, for you will be separated from His way. This has He instructed you that you may become righteous' (Quran 6:153); '... so whoever wills – let him believe; and whoever wills – let him disbelieve' (Quran 18:29); 'And whoever commits a sin only earns it against himself' (Quran 4:111); 'So whoever does an atom's weight of good will see it, And whoever does an atom's weight of evil will see it' (Quran 99:7–8); 'Whoever does righteousness – it is for his [own] soul; and whoever does evil [does so] against it. And your Lord is not ever unjust to [His] servants' (Quran 41:46), and others.

In contrast, the *jabriyya* emerged as a counter-argument, rejecting the notion of human choice. They, too, referred to Quranic verses to support their stance, such as: 'Allah has set a seal upon their hearts and upon their hearing, and over their vision is a veil. And for them is a great punishment' (quran 2:7); 'And my advice will not benefit you – although I wished to advise you – If Allah should intend to put you in error. He is your Lord, and to Him you will be returned' (Quran 11:34); 'And We certainly sent into every nation a messenger, [saying], "Worship Allah and avoid Taghut." And among them were those whom Allah guided, and among them were those upon whom error was [deservedly] decreed' (Quran 16:36), and others.

The Prophet's companions, along with the advocates of *athariyya*,[3] fiercely opposed the *qadariyya*, deeming it blasphemous. This opposition gained the support of the Umayyad dynasty, which viewed the *qadariyya* as aligning with its political adversaries. Conversely, the Umayyads favored the *jabriyya*, considering it an ideological pillar that endorsed the notion of predestination – where man has no control over his actions – and was thus destined to triumph. The Umayyad rulers persecuted *qadariyya* leaders, such as Maʿbad ibn Khalid al-Juhani, who was crucified by Al-Hajjaj on the order of Caliph ʿAbd

2 Al-Shmali n.d., p. 133.

3 *Athariyya* (from Arabic *athar*, meaning "tradition") refers to a traditionalist school of Islamic theology that emphasises strict adherence to the Quran and Hadith, rejecting speculative theology (*kalam*) and philosophical reasoning in favor of literal interpretation of scriptural texts, notably associated with scholars like Ahmad ibn Hanbal. (A.K.)

al-Malik ibn Marwan (r. 685–705 CE),[4] and his disciple Ghaylan al-Dimashqi, whose hands and feet were severed before he was executed and crucified on the orders of Caliph Hisham ibn ʿAbd al-Malik (r. 705–15).

Despite serving the Umayyad agenda, the *jabriyya* opened the door for rebellion. Some rebels interpreted the foundational concept of *jabriyya* to mean that their revolt was also predestined by God, with no human control over it. Thus Jahm ibn Safwan – one of the most prominent *jabriyya* thinkers and founder of the faction later known as the *jahmiyya* – took part in the uprising of the Khurasani leader al-Harith ibn Surayj al-Farisi[5] in 116 AH / 734 CE against Caliph Hisham ibn ʿAbd al-Malik. Hisham's reign was marked by the unprecedented territorial expansion of the Arab-Islamic empire, stretching from the Atlantic Ocean in the west to Central Asia in the east – surpassing the Roman Empire in geographical scope. Historians often regard his era as the 'golden age' of the Umayyads or the peak of their imperial grandeur. Yet this political zenith was accompanied by deepening social inequality, and the vast conquests intensified resistance among subjugated peoples. Accordingly, alongside military victories, the Umayyad era witnessed numerous sociopolitical uprisings, including the revolt of al-Harith ibn Surayj and Jahm ibn Safwan.

Historians emphasise that al-Harith's rebellion against Hisham was couched in religious slogans and framed as a defense of Islam – an indication that the *jahmiyya* wing of the *jabriyya* was hostile to the Umayyads. This can be attributed to the *jahmiyya*'s willingness to employ allegorical interpretation (*taʾwil*) without restraint, as the *qadariyya* had done. Jahm himself espoused the view that Paradise and Hell are not eternal, on the grounds that only God is eternal. In the same period, Jaʿd ibn Dirham – the leader of the *jabriyya* in its formative stage – asserted the createdness of the Quran,[6] reasoning that to affirm the Quran's eternity would be to posit a co-eternal alongside God, which he considered impossible.

4 Al-Shmali n.d., p. 133.

5 Al-Harith ibn Surayj (d. 746 CE) was a prominent Arab rebel leader in Khurasan who led uprisings against Umayyad rule from 734–46 CE, advocating for the 'Book of God and the Sunna of His Prophet' and social justice, and whose movement contributed to the weakening of Umayyad power before the Abbasid revolution. (A.K.)

6 In his book *Tarikh al-Falsafa al-ʿArabiyya al-Islamiyya*, ʿAbdo Al-Shmali explains the concept of the Quran's createdness, clarifying that some factions argued that speech, a requirement for the Quran, is not an independent attribute of God, as it necessitates physical organs.

2 The Emergence of the Muʿtazila and their Views

In this climate of intellectual discourse, shaped by various socio-religious movements such as the Kharijites, the Shiʿa, and the Murjiʾa, the Muʿtazila emerged. Historians estimate that it arose during the reign of the Umayyad Caliph Hisham ibn Abd al-Malik (724–43 CE / 106–26 AH).

Older and more recent scholars have disagreed over the origin of the name 'Muʿtazilites' (literally, separatists). It is commonly argued that the movement's founders, Wasil ibn ʿAtaʾ and ʿAmr ibn ʿUbayd, distanced themselves from the intellectual circle of the prominent thinker Hasan al-Basri after disagreeing with him on a crucial theological point. Specifically, they rejected his view that a person who commits a major sin is neither a true believer nor a disbeliever, but occupies an intermediate position. This disagreement, it is claimed, led to their being called Muʿtazilites. The name allegedly arose because they 'took a position different from the mainstream', distancing themselves from the prevailing opinions on major sinners: while the Murjiʾa held that such individuals remained believers, the Azariqa (a Kharijite faction) deemed them disbelievers, and Hasan al-Basri considered them hypocrites (*munafiqun*).[7] Wasil, in contrast, argued that they were neither believers nor disbelievers.[8]

Regardless of whether the name Muʿtazilites refers to a formal incident – departing from a scholarly circle – or to a deeper ideological divergence, it is clear that Muʿtazilism emerged during a significant historical period. This era was characterised by the stability of the Umayyad Caliphate on the one hand, and by ongoing social and ethnic rebellions on the other.

This context suggests that the Muʿtazilites initially arose as an intellectual movement in opposition to radical Shiʿa and Kharijite factions, as well as to anti-Islamic ideologies that were often labeled as *zandaqa*[9] (heresy). In his work *Al-Munya wa Al-Amal* (Wish and Hope), Al-Murtada[10] documented the

7 *Munafiq* (plural: munafiqun) is an Arabic term meaning 'hypocrite', referring in Islamic context to those who outwardly profess Islam while secretly harboring disbelief or working against the Muslim community, as described in the Quran, particularly regarding certain inhabitants of Medina during Prophet Muhammad's time.

8 Amin 1964, 288–9.

9 Later, the term *Zandaqa* emerged, attributed to those who criticised rulers and the founders of more liberal schools of thought.

10 ʿAli ibn al-Husayn al-Sharif al-Murtada (966–1044 CE) was a prominent Shia scholar, theologian, and poet in Baghdad, known for his works on Islamic jurisprudence, theology, and literature, including *Al-Shafi fi al-Imama* and *Al-Munya wa al-Amal*, and considered one of the leading intellectual figures of the Buyid period.

words of Wasil ibn ʿAta''s followers: 'No one was more knowledgeable than he (Wasil) in the discourse of the extremist Shiʿa, the seceding Kharijites, the heretical *zanadaqa* and *dahriyya*, the Murji'a, and all other opponents – and in refuting them'.[11]

The *Concise Islamic Encyclopedia* notes that one of the fundamental principles of the Muʿtazila was their struggle against *zandaqa* (heresy) and *thanawiyya* (dualism) – the latter being rooted in Persian Manichaeism[12] and based on the belief in two deities, Light and Darkness, or Good and Evil.

Thus, the Muʿtazila constituted an intellectual current that confronted what would be (at that time) described as 'dangerous' social movements, yet remained firmly within the framework of Islam. For this reason, the Muʿtazilites did not come into conflict with the Umayyad regime – particularly since they also refrained from taking part in the struggle between the Umayyads and the Shiʿa, as well as between the Umayyads and the Kharijites. Indeed, some sources report that the name 'Muʿtazila' was given to them because they 'withdrew' (*iʿtazala*), refusing to pledge allegiance to ʿAli; they also stood aside from the two warring factions – ʿAlī on the one hand, and ʿA'isha, Talha, and al-Zubayr on the other.[13]

Scholars have argued that the Muʿtazilites' criticism of both Ali and Muʿawiya brought them closer to the Umayyads, who found it advantageous to equate the two figures. Consequently, some later Umayyad caliphs, such as Yazid ibn al-Walid (744 CE / 127 AH) and Marwan ibn Muhammad (744–50 CE / 127–33 AH), were inclined towards Muʿtazila.[14] This, however, did not prevent the Muʿtazila from supporting the ʿAbbasids and advocating for their cause, so that under al-Ma'mun – the golden age of the ʿAbbasid dynasty – Muʿtazilism became the official ideology of the caliphate.

It is certain that Muʿtazilism, which originated under the Umayyads and developed under the ʿAbbasids, crystallised into five fundamental principles. These principles led some early writers to refer to the Muʿtazila as *ahl al-usul al-khamsa* (the people of the five principles). The five principles consisted of: the affirmation of divine unity (*tawhid*), divine justice (*ʿadl*), the promise and the threat (*al-waʿd wa-l-waʿid*), the intermediate position (*al-manzila bayna*

---

11 Amin 1933, vol. 3, p. 97.

12 See note 56.

13 Aisha, the Prophet's wife, allied with Talha and Zubair, who sought to gain the Caliphate, and fought against Ali, who defeated them in the Battle of the Camel. During the battle, Aisha remained in a howdah, urging her allies to fight, until her camel was injured, bringing her to the ground.

14 Amin 1964, p. 295.

al-manzilatayn), and the enjoining of right and forbidding of wrong (*al-amr bi-l-maʿruf wa-l-nahy ʿan al-munkar*).

These principles blend religious thought with philosophical analysis, as the Muʿtazilites were philosophers who sought to reconcile philosophy with religion by providing rational explanations. Thus, their call to affirm divine unity (*tawhid*) – which is not only among the foundations of Islam but its essential core – took a distinctly philosophical turn. They embraced the doctrine of transcendence (*tanzih*) and interpreted Quranic verses that describe God in anthropomorphic terms, such as 'The Most Merciful [who is] above the Throne established' (*thumma istawa ʿala al-ʿarsh*), (Quran 20:5) through allegorical exegesis (*taʾwil*). They held, for example, that 'God is one, nothing is like Him; He is not a body, not a phantom, not a substance, not an image, not flesh nor blood, not a person nor an essence … He has no length, breadth, or depth'. This perspective was based on the Quranic verse: '… There is nothing like unto Him …' (Quran 42:11). Accordingly, they denied any physical attributes assigned to God, as doing so would imply that His existence could be concretely described. This would contradict Muʿtazilite's *tawhid*, which held that God is an independent entity whose being and knowledge are not external to His existence but integral to it, and that He transcends all materiality.

From this understanding, the Muʿtazilite doctrine of *qadariyya* (freedom of choice) became a crucial part of their belief system. They denied that God could commit injustice, arguing that 'injustice comes only from a person who is compelled by need or from someone ignorant who does not know that injustice is wrong and thus commits it without understanding its implications'.[15] Based on their monotheistic perspective, the Muʿtazila also accepted the doctrine of the 'created Quran' (*khalq al-Quran*). For them, the Quran could not be eternal, coexisting with God since pre-eternity, for that would imply a second eternal being alongside Him. Rather, it is God's speech brought into existence as a created act (*makhluq*), manifested in another – namely, the Prophet Muhammad.

The denial of the Quran's eternity was of great importance, as it opened the door to research, analysis, and the examination of religious texts without fanaticism or narrow-mindedness. Since the Quran was seen as a creation of God meant to address the needs of humankind and its era, its interpretation could evolve to align with contemporary developments. Their concept of justice, the second most important Muʿtazilite principle, was humanistic and built on three key ideas: God guides humanity towards a goal and desires only good for His creation, as He neither wills evil nor commands it; God is not the author

---

15 Amin 1964, p. 31.

of humankind's good or evil deeds, for human will is free, and people are the creators of their actions. The significance of this position lay in the rejection of the idea that evil in the world was predetermined, as their adversaries claimed. Instead, the Muʿtazilites argued that evil was a creation of society, which could be corrected.

When some Muʿtazilites addressed the relationship between God and society, they not only asserted that God wanted to improve the conditions of humanity, but also that He should do what is best for humanity.[16] In line with the justice principle, they explored the nature of desirable and detestable actions. They argued that human reason could differentiate between good and evil, as justice, honesty, courage, and generosity are inherently positive traits, while oppression, cowardice, lies, and miserliness are inherently negative. They refuted their adversaries' claims that *sharia* alone determined what is desirable and detestable, emphasising that human beings, even before the advent of *sharia*, judged actions through reason and discovered the moral value of deeds based on logical thinking. For example, *sharia* protected souls and property because of their intrinsic good, and it prohibited killing and theft because of the inherent evil in such actions.[17]

It is evident that the Muʿtazilites aimed to highlight the supremacy of reason. However, in this endeavor, they limited themselves to the values of the social class to which they belonged, failing to recognise that moral values and social laws are tightly linked to the dominant class-based power structures, which differ according to the dominant social classes. Even universal values such as honesty and courage take on different meanings depending on the social class that discusses them. For instance, the protection of wealth in class-based societies differs markedly from that in non-class-based societies.

Nonetheless, the Muʿtazilites' support for the existing regime does not undermine their contribution to the glorification of reason, as they argued that 'its only limits are its evidence, and once the evidence is validated, there is no room for error'.[18] Muʿtazilism also paved the way for thinkers like the Muʿtazilite philosopher Abu Ishaq Ibrahim ibn Sayyar ibn Hani al-Nazzam, who preceded the European philosophers of the eighteenth century. He asserted that 'the doubter is closer to the truth than the denier, for one cannot attain certainty without doubt, and whenever one changes one's position, some doubt must be involved'.

16 Amin 1964, p. 45.
17 Amin 1964, p. 47.
18 Al-Shmali n.d., p. 201.

Given this, all philosophical conclusions should be subject to debate and discussion. An-Naẓẓām (d. in 221 AH / 835 CE), who lived in the third century AH (ninth century CE), during the Golden Abbasid era, represented the high-level liberal thinking that characterised the Muʿtazilite school at its peak.

Thus, the three remaining Muʿtazilite principles – the promise and the threat (*al-waʿd wa-l-waʿid*), the intermediate position (*al-manzila bayna al-manzilatayn*), and the enjoining of right and forbidding of wrong (*al-amr bi-l-maʿruf wa-l-nahy ʿan al-munkar*) – can be seen as faith-based principles rooted in their religious and ethical views, particularly their notions of justice and the rational organisation of society.

While 'the promise and the threat' dealt with minor and major sins, 'the intermediate position' addressed the status of those who committed these sins, and 'enjoining the right and forbidding the wrong' focused on the relationship with the government. This principle was derived from the Quran, particularly the verse: 'And let there be [arising] from you a nation inviting to [all that is] good, enjoining what is right and forbidding what is wrong, and those will be the successful' (Quran 3:104). The Muʿtazilites believed that wrongs should be forbidden through the heart, words, and, if necessary, action, including the use of the sword if other methods failed. This interpretation was based on the verse: 'And if two factions among the believers should fight, then make settlement between them. But if one of them oppresses the other, then fight against the one that oppresses until it returns to the ordinance of Allah' (Quran 49:9). In this respect, they aligned with the Kharijites but differed in their approach. While the Kharijites saw *enjoining the right* as an individual obligation (*fard ʿayn*),[19] the Muʿtazilites considered it a communal duty (*fard kifaya*).[20] Thus, the Kharijites went to war regardless of the consequences,[21] whereas the Muʿtazilites, guided by reason, avoided unnecessary violence.

The Muʿtazilites' stance on this issue shaped their position in society. The association of some Umayyad caliphs, particularly al-Maʾmun (r. 813–33 CE), with this school of thought, and its adoption as the official ideology of the

19 *Fard ʿayn* is an Islamic legal term referring to individual religious obligations that are binding on every capable Muslim personally, such as the five daily prayers, fasting during Ramadan, and the pilgrimage to Mecca, as distinguished from *fard kifaya* (collective obligations). (A.K.)

20 *Fard kifaya* is an Islamic legal term referring to collective religious obligations that are binding on the Muslim community as a whole, but if fulfilled by some members, the obligation is lifted from others, such as funeral prayers, seeking knowledge, or defending Muslim lands. (A.K.)

21 Amin n.d., vol. 3, p. 67.

Abbasid state, made it difficult for Muʿtazilism to function as a revolutionary opposition within the ruling elite. Under these conditions, Muʿtazilism became the ideology of the Islamic Arab Empire during its period of rapid growth and socioeconomic prosperity. However, as uneven development and social-ethnic conflicts arose, the Muʿtazilites were influenced by these changes. Some aligned with the Shiʿites, and in Tahert (near Tlemcen in the Maghreb), they even allied with the Kharijites and rebelled against al-Mansur, the second Abbasid caliph.

Nevertheless, Muʿtazilism as a whole functioned as the ideology of the ruling class, composed of merchants, large landowners, and the wealthy – at least for as long as this class was in ascendance. From this social base the movement acquired its progressive character. Yet, the triumph of the Muʿtazila under the caliph al-Ma'mun marked the beginning of their departure from certain progressive features. This was most evident in the attempt, guided by state authority, to impose the doctrine of the created Quran upon the people by force. Such enforcement led to the persecution and even execution of numerous intellectuals (including leading Sunni scholars) who refused to accept the doctrine and insisted instead on the Quran's eternity.

The conduct of the Muʿtazila in this period starkly contradicted their earlier commitment to tolerance, for it is in the very nature of an ideology – once adopted by a dominant class – to harden into coercion. Having once defended human intellectual freedom and upheld the practice of free disputation in the pursuit of truth, the Muʿtazila abandoned both freedom and rational debate once they assumed political power. This period was justly described by contemporaries as the *mihna* (the 'ordeal' or 'inquisition'). In truth, it was a trial in more than one sense: it was the ordeal of their opponents, the ordeal of reason itself, and a turning point that provoked resistance and ultimately led to the decline of Muʿtazilism under the caliph al-Mutawakkil (r. 232–247 AH / 847–861 CE). In the second year of his reign, al-Mutawakkil ordered an end to the *mihna* and banned further discussion of the question of the Quran's createdness.

Al-Mutawakkil's position served the Sunnis, gradually empowering them until the emergence of Abu Hasan al-Ashʿari (260–325 AH / 873–936 CE). Al-Ashʿari refined their position through philosophical argumentation, helping them overcome the Muʿtazilites and providing the rulers with a traditional conservative ideology. This ideological alignment coincided with the onset of the decline of the Islamic Arab Empire.

The rigid nature of al-Ashʿari's thought is clearly illustrated in the following passage from his book *Al-Ibana fi Usul al-Diyana* (The Clarification of the Fundamentals of Religion), where he discusses Muʿtazilism:

> God created all things by His power and governs them according to His will. However, many Muʿtazilites and proponents of *qadariyya* followed their predecessors blindly, interpreting the Quran according to their own views rather than as it was revealed by God. They neither had any proof granted by God nor did they interpret it as conveyed by the Prophet or understood by the early Muslims. They opposed the teachings of the Prophet's companions regarding the vision of God on the Day of Judgment. Furthermore, they denied the Prophet's intercession (Shafaʿa) and the Punishment of the Grave, rejecting the belief – agreed upon by the companions and their successors – that all infidels are punished in their graves. They also subscribed to the belief in the Quran's createdness, denying it as God's eternal word, which aligned them ideologically with the polytheists. They argued that humans create evil, much like the Zoroastrians, who believed in two gods: one who creates good and one who creates evil. Moreover, the advocates of *qadariyyah* claimed that while God creates goodness, Satan creates evil. They went further, asserting that God could desire something that does not ultimately occur, and that things could happen contrary to God's will – opinions that contradict the consensus of the Muslim community and the clear words of the Quran: 'And you do not will except that Allah wills' (Quran 76:30).

It can be concluded that al-Ashʿari and his counter-school of thought effectively ended the era of independent reasoning and analysis, opting instead for strict adherence to the original religious texts. The Ashʿarite school triumphed over other intellectual approaches, not because of its capacity to address contemporary issues, but by reinforcing the established order. During the tenth century CE (fourteenth century AH), the system was not receptive to the rationalist tendencies of the Muʿtazili tes, who, as previously noted, exhibited a degree of fanaticism.

The dominance of Al-Ashʿari's thought, or the Sunnite rationale, was a significant blow to the enlightened and liberal Islamic-Arab intellectual tradition. Liberal scholars are right to assert that the defeat of the Muʿtazilites deprived ideological freedom of its principal foundation, stifled intellectual engagement, and subordinated the mind to tradition, thus putting an end to rational critique and debate. In this context, Ahmad Amin observed:

> I believe that if the Muʿtazilite principles have prevailed – particularly in regard to the sovereignty of reason and the affirmation of free will – Muslims would have held a different position and significance in history than they do today. Subjugation has paralyzed them, and dependency has rendered them powerless.[22]

22 Amin n.d., p. 70.

He further added:

> The downfall of the Muʿtazilites led Muslims into a prolonged period of intellectual stagnation, under the influence of conservative thought, which lasted for more than a millennium until the advent of the modern renaissance.[23]

It is important to recognise that the Muʿtazilites represented a phase of historical renaissance, much like how bourgeois democracy marked a period of political and socio-economic prosperity in history. Just as progressive bourgeois thought declined with the end of its prosperity phase and was replaced by reactionary, fanatical ideologies during the decline of capitalism, Ashʿarism replaced Muʿtazilism as the Islamic Arab Empire began its regression.

23 Amin n.d., p. 207.

CHAPTER 6

Al-Ashʿariyya: The Ideology of the Feudal Era

1 The Era of Al-Mutawakkil as a Turning Point

Historians agree that Abu al-Fadl Jaʿfar ibn al-Mutawakkil ʿala Allah (r. 232–47 AH / 847–61 CE) was instrumental in helping the traditional school of thought (the Sunnite school) regain its former status. He ordered the cessation of discussions and debates and commanded people to adhere strictly to traditions. He also dismissed liberal thinkers from official positions and halted lectures in the fields of science and philosophy. Furthermore, he 'went further and persecuted the *dhimmi*s (non-Muslims),[1] who endured some of the harshest forms of injustice during his Caliphate, as they were removed from official positions and stripped of all privileges'.[2]

From this, it appears that al-Mutawakkil sought to resolve the ideological dispute between the Muʿtazilites and the advocates of the traditional school at an administrative and official level. For this reason, and others, some historians referred to him as 'The Arab Nero', implying that the intellectual 'imperial overthrow' was tied to this tyrannical Caliph.

In truth, this Caliph was not markedly different from his predecessors. He continued their legacy, and in his violent practices, followed in the footsteps of his great-grandfather, Abu al-Abbas as-Saffah (r. 132–63 AH / 749–54 CE), the founder of the dynasty. It is evident that the seeds of ideological decline began during the era of Abu Jaʿfar Harun al-Wathiq bi-Llah (r. 227–32 AH / 842–47 CE). Despite his positive approach and commitment to freedom of thought, he failed to spread his principles effectively, as the judiciary and men of authority obstructed his efforts, paving the way for the resurgence of reactionary ideas. Against this backdrop, al-Mutawakkil rose to power and issued his 'intellectual commands'. It thus becomes evident that the issue is not subjective but objective, and that the role of individuals – despite its importance – is not decisive in itself. Rather, its impact is determined by the extent to which it aligns with

1 The term *dhimmi* (pl. *dhimmis*) refers to non-Muslim subjects – primarily Christians, Jews, and later Zoroastrians – living under Islamic rule who were granted protection (*dhimma*) in exchange for acknowledging Muslim political authority and paying a special tax (*jizya*). While theoretically afforded security of life and property, their status was legally and socially subordinate to that of Muslims. (A.K.)

2 Ali 1938.

 HTTPS://DOI.ORG/10.1163/9789004774261-011

socio-political development. Ideas, in this sense, reflect the conditions of a given society and embody the positions of its class forces at specific historical junctures.

While al-Mutawakkil supported the traditional (Sunnite) school of thought, and is considered by some a pivotal figure, the triumph of Sunnite ideology was a process that spanned more than half a century. It was closely associated with the principles of Abu Hasan al-Ashʿari (260–325 AH / 873–936 CE). During this period, social conflicts intensified, influencing the approaches of al-Mutawakkil and his successors. It is important to highlight some of the causes of these conflicts and their dangerous consequences.

One of the most significant conflicts was the class struggle that arose from deep social polarisation between the wealthy and the poor. Although precise statistics reflecting the deep class divisions are scarce, information about properties confiscated by the Caliphs from affluent individuals demonstrates the great disparity between the two classes. In his book *Muhadarat Tarikh al-Umam al-Islamiyyah* (The Abbasid State), Sheikh Muhammad al-Khudari[3] noted that:

> Al-Mutawakkil confiscated the properties of the chief advisor (Wazir or minister – E.T.) Umar ibn Faraj al-Rakhji and his brother Muhammad, amounting to 240,000 dinars[4] and 15,000 dirhams, in addition to his palace, belongings, and estate. The transport of his possessions required fifty camels, making multiple trips.[5]

This illustrates how social inequality was intensified under his reign, as most people at the time were suffering from poverty, with incomes amounting to only a few dirhams.

It is worth noting that this chief advisor was not among the wealthiest, owning money, land, and slaves, but was rather from the middle class. It is not surprising, then, that revolutionary class conflict shifted from the periphery to the center. As a result, during this period, the locus of

3 Muhammad al-Khudari (1872–1927) was a modern Islamic historian and scholar known for his multi-volume work *Muhadarat fi Tarikh al-Umam al-Islamiyya* ("Lectures on the History of Islamic Nations"), which covers the political, social, and military history of the Islamic world from the early caliphates through the Abbasid period. (A.K.)

4 The dinar was the primary gold currency of the Islamic world, originally based on the Byzantine solidus and standardised under the Umayyad caliph Abd al-Malik ibn Marwan (685–705 CE), serving as the foundation of medieval Islamic monetary systems alongside the silver dirham. (A.K.)

5 Al-Khudari n.d., p. 256.

revolutionary class struggle shifted from the peripheries to the very heart of the empire. Al-Mutawakkil, who ascended the caliphal throne in the same year that the central authority succeeded in suppressing the Babak al-Khurrami revolt in the northern frontier regions, lived long enough to sense the early rumblings of the Zanj uprising. This latter revolt erupted in Khuzistan, near the seat of the caliphate, during the reign of his successor al-Muʿtazz (r. 252–55 AH / 866–68 CE).

The two revolutions complemented each other. Babak al-Khurrami, who began his revolutionary movement in Azerbaijan in the summer of 201 AH / 816 CE, sought to redistribute land to peasants, freeing them from the tyranny of landlords and feudal lords. Similarly, ʿAli ibn Muhammad al-Barquʿi, the leader of the Zanj Rebellion, sought to liberate slaves from the burdens of harsh slavery.[6]

In these circumstances, marked by the widening gulf between rulers and the mass of the ruled, it was hardly surprising that the caliphs refrained from recruiting Arabs or Persians into their armies and instead turned to mercenaries, especially Turks, to form military units tasked with defending the regime both internally and externally. Although the recruitment of Turks had begun under al-Ma'mun (r. 198–218 AH / 813–33 CE), it was his successor, the caliph Abu Ishaq Muhammad al-Muʿtasim bi-llah (r. 218–27 AH / 833–42 CE), who transformed this quantitative measure into a qualitative one, making the Turkish military corps decisive. Historians generally agree that with this step al-Muʿtasim committed a grave error, for he thereby weakened the authority of the caliphate and undermined its foundations. The rupture between rulers and ruled was further reinforced when the caliph, accompanied by his Turkish guard, moved the seat of government from Baghdad to Samarra' (*Surr man ra'a*, 'He who sees it rejoices'), after growing discontent among the capital's inhabitants over the conduct of these mercenary soldiers and al-Muʿtasim's fear of an imminent popular uprising.

Al-Khudari wrote in this regard: 'Al-Muʿtasim alone bears the greater responsibility for the turmoil that later befell the ʿAbbasids, for the weakening of their authority, and for the calamity that struck the Arab umma through the dominance of this foreign element over its affairs.' (4).[7] He added that the arrogance

6 These two revolutions will be further discussed within the framework of the research on social revolutions in the Islamic Arab Empire.

7 This assessment reflects a later Arab-centric historiographical perspective, emphasising the perceived dangers of relying on non-Arab (in this case, Turkish) mercenary forces. Modern scholars note that such interpretations often project later notions of Arab political primacy onto earlier periods and should be contextualised within both the socio-political realities of

of one of these soldiers led to the revolt of Abu Harb al-Mubarqaʿ al-Yamani in Palestine,[8] and the popular nature of this revolt was evident in its participants, most of whom were peasants.[9] Soon, the true nature of these mercenary brigades became clear, as they followed the example of the chiefs of the imperial guard in ancient Rome, supporting some Caliphs and overthrowing them to serve their own interests. Al-Mutawakkil was the first Caliph to gain power by the sword of the Turkish commanders, despite opposition from the statesmen, chief judge, and chief advisors. He was also the first to be assassinated by these same commanders.

The social conflicts and the decline of the Caliphate's authority led to the expansion of feudalism on the one hand, and the independence of provincial governors from Baghdad on the other. Various historians have noted this, one of whom wrote:

> The tumults that prevailed in the state after the death of al-Muntasir[10] encouraged the governors to gradually achieve independence in their provinces, rendering them owners of feudal estates rather than officials following the Caliph's orders. This undermined the Caliphate's authority, leaving it with nothing but its name.[11]

It appears that the growth of the *iqtaʿ* system, which accompanied the increasing independence of the provinces from the caliphate, accelerated during the reign of al-Ma'mun. In return for the support of Persian notables in his conflict with his brother al-Amin, al-Ma'mun granted them vast tracts of land in Khurasan. This led to the rise of the Tahirid family, whose rule in the northeastern provinces began under ʿAbd Allah ibn Tahir (r. 213–30 AH / 828–44 CE) and lasted until 260 AH / 873 CE, when Yaʿqub ibn al-Layth al-Saffār defeated the Tahirids' last ruler and established the Saffarid dynasty in Sijistan, Khurasan, and Tabaristan.[12]

---

the 9th-century Abbasid state and the subsequent historiographical agenda of commentators like al-Khudari. (A.K.)

8 The soldier assaulted the wife of Abu Harb, prompting him to retaliate by killing the soldier and fleeing to the mountains of Jordan.

9 Al-Khudari n.d., p. 241.

10 Al-Muntasir (r. 861–62 CE) was the Abbasid caliph who succeeded his father al-Mutawakkil after the latter's assassination. His reign was brief and largely overshadowed by the growing dominance of Turkish military commanders, whose influence in court politics undermined the authority of the caliphate. (A.K.)

11 Ali 1938, p. 249.

12 The Tahirids (821–73 CE) were a Persian dynasty that ruled Khurasan nominally on behalf

During this time, the feudal Samanid Emirate[13] emerged in Transoxiana (Central Asia), with Ismail-i Samani, a prominent figure, coming to power in 279 AH / 892 CE. Ismail-i Samani separated the provinces he united from the Caliphate's control. Al-Khudari noted the feudal fragmentation that affected the Islamic Arab Empire, highlighting that the provinces or states that coexisted during the period of Al-Mutawakkil included the Idrisids[14] in Morocco, the Aghlabids[15] in Tunisia and Algeria, the Ziyadids in Yemen, and the Tahirids in Khorasan.[16]

This was followed by the establishment of the Tulunid state, named after its founder Ahmad ibn Tulun, in Egypt. The state later annexed Damascus (Syria) and lasted from 254–293 AH / 868–905 CE. It became evident that a close connection existed between the provinces' independence from the Caliphate and the development of feudalism, particularly in terms of land ownership and the peasants' ties to the land. This dynamic was exemplified in Tabaristan, where Muhammad ibn Tahir seized lands that, until 250 AH / 864 CE, had been collectively held by peasants, ultimately sparking a popular rebellion.

Ibn al-Athir recounts in his *al-Kamil fī al-tarikh* this exemplary incident of the spread of feudalism. He wrote that al-Hasan ibn Zayd al-ʿAlawi al-Shiʿi (who led the uprising) revolted in the districts of Tabaristan. The cause of his revolt, Ibn al-Athir explains, was that al-Mustaʿin[17] granted to Muhammad ibn Tahir portions of the Caliphate's crown lands (*sawafi al-sultan*)[18] in Tabaristan. Among these grants was an estate near the frontiers of Tabaristan, in the dis-

of the Abbasid caliphs, though in practice they enjoyed broad autonomy. They were succeeded by the Saffarids (861–1003 CE), a dynasty founded by Yaʿqub ibn al-Layth al-Saffar, a former coppersmith turned military leader, who extended his authority over Sijistan, Khurasan, and parts of Iran, marking a decisive shift toward independent regional rule in the Islamic East.

13 The Samanid Emirate (819–999 CE) was a Persian dynasty that ruled Transoxiana and Khurasan under nominal Abbasid suzerainty. Ismaʿil b. Ahmad (Ismaʿil-i Samani, r. 892–907 CE) consolidated the dynasty's power, making Bukhara a flourishing political and cultural center, particularly of Persian literature and science. (A.K.)

14 The Idrisids (789–974 CE) were a Shiʿi dynasty founded by Idris I, a descendant of Hasan b. Ali, in Morocco. They represented one of the earliest independent Shiʿi states in the Islamic West. (A.K.)

15 The Aghlabids (800–909 CE), a semi-independent dynasty under Abbasid suzerainty, ruled Ifrīqiya (modern Tunisia, eastern Algeria, and western Libya). They are notable for their naval campaigns and the conquest of Sicily (827 CE). (A.K.)

16 Ali 1938, p. 255.

17 Al-Mustaʿin bi-llah (r. 862–66 CE) was an ʿAbbasid caliph whose reign was marked by instability and the growing influence of Turkish military commanders.

18 The term *sawafi al-sultan* refers to crown lands or state-owned estates whose revenues went directly to the caliphal treasury. (A.K.)

tricts of Daylam (south of the Caspian Sea). Adjacent to this estate lay lands belonging collectively to the local inhabitants, which included their woodlands, pastures for their livestock, and common lands for their livelihood. No individual had private ownership over them. Muhammad ibn Tahir dispatched one of his clerks to take possession of the land granted to him. When his envoy attempted to claim not only the estate itself but also the adjacent communal lands (*al-mawat*) from which the locals derived their livelihood, the people of that region refused to hand them over – so they revolted.[19]

Likewise, one of the outcomes of the Zanj Rebellion was the liberation of slaves and the transformation of the productive relations in Kalda (southern Iraq) into a feudal relationship between landowners and peasants. This meant that the newly freed slaves became peasants who were strongly bound to the land, though this bond did not develop into a legal attachment as in European feudalism, where the peasant was considered part of the land and forbidden to leave it. It was only natural that the spread of feudalism and regional fragmentation would weaken the central authority in two key domains: finances and the labor force.

The independence of the provinces deprived the Caliphate, sometimes entirely and sometimes partially, of the *kharaj* (land tax), which amounted to hundreds of millions of dirhams. It also disrupted trade and industry, transforming the economy – under conditions of regional isolation – into an agrarian system on the one hand and a craft-based economy, including domestic industries, on the other. Moreover, the central authority lost the support of the local populations in these provinces and became entirely dependent on mercenary military units, which evolved into an internal plundering apparatus, especially since they were neither native to the country nor integrated into its economic and social life.

This was exemplified by the rebellion of Turkish soldiers during the reign of Al-Muʿtazz in 255 AH / 868 CE, when their riots escalated, and they demanded the Caliph pay their wages. When 'he told them that the state treasury was empty, they forced him to leave the palace and began beating and insulting him, until he was compelled to abdicate. They later assassinated him after imprisoning him for a time'.[20]

Over time, the Caliphate of Baghdad became not only a nominal entity but also a historical paradox, as it was controlled by more powerful states. To consider it a continuation of the Islamic Arab Empire would be an absurd-

19 Ibn al-Athir, *Al-Kamil fi al-Tarikh*, vol. 7, quoted in Farah 1962, p. 157.

20 Ali 1938, p. 250.

ity. Among the most significant of these successor states, particularly in terms of supporting the Sunni Ashʿarite school of thought, was the Seljuk Empire,[21] which inherited the Ghaznavid Empire[22] in the fifth century AH / eleventh century CE. When Alp Arslan[23] ascended the Seljuk throne in 454 AH / 1062 CE, and Nizam al-Mulk[24] was appointed chief advisor, Ashʿarism became the official ideology. It was disseminated throughout Muslim territories, becoming an entrenched religious doctrine. 'When Salah al-Din al-Ayyubi[25] came into power in the twelfth century, Ashʿarism spread widely across Africa, particularly in Egypt, as well as in Morocco and most Islamic countries'.[26]

2 Two Factors in the Development of Ashʿarism

Abu al-Hasan Ali ibn Ismail al-Ashʿari was born in Basra in 260 AH / 873 CE to a family descended from Abu Musa al-Ashʿari, one of the mediators in the Battle of Siffin between Alī ibn Abī Ṭālib and Muʿawiya, the Umayyad governor of Damascus. Raised in a Muʿtazilite intellectual environment, his stepfather, Muhammad ibn ʿAbd al-Wahhab al-Jubba'i, was the Muʿtazilite leader of the time and a prominent scholar in Muʿtazilite philosophy.

Two factors proved decisive in al-Ashʿari's intellectual development and his eventual break with the Muʿtazilites, after being one of their prominent advocates. The first was objective, linked to the conditions of the Islamic Arab Empire, which was experiencing escalating violent social conflict that threatened the entire socioeconomic structure. The Qarmatian revolution, which

21 The Seljuk Empire (1037–1194 CE) was a Sunni Muslim Turkish dynasty that at its height controlled much of Central Asia, the Iranian plateau, Anatolia, and parts of the Levant and Arabian Peninsula. (A.K.)

22 The Ghaznavid Empire (977–1186 CE) was a Persianate Muslim dynasty that controlled parts of present-day Afghanistan, Pakistan, and northern India. The Seljuks gradually absorbed Ghaznavid territories beginning in the early 11th century. (A.K.)

23 Alp Arslan (r. 1063–72 CE) was the second sultan of the Seljuk Empire, known for his military campaigns and the decisive victory over the Byzantine Empire at the Battle of Manzikert in 1071 CE. (A.K.)

24 Abu Ali al-Hasan ibn Ali Tusi, known as Nizam al-Mulk (1018–1092 CE), was a Persian scholar and vizier who served as the chief minister to both Alp Arslan and his successor Malik-Shah I. He established the Nizamiyyah madrasas to promote orthodox Sunni education. (A.K.)

25 Salah al-Din Yusuf ibn Ayyub, known in the West as Saladin (1137–1193 CE), was the founder of the Ayyubid dynasty and sultan of Egypt and Syria. He is famous for his role in the Crusades and his recapture of Jerusalem from the Crusader states in 1187 CE. (A.K.)

26 Al-Shmali n.d., p. 220.

erupted in 278 AH / 891 CE during al-Ashʿari's youth, threatened the class system with its humanistic principles and calls for equality, as well as its economic organisation, which aimed at liberating peasants and workers. This frightened al-Ashʿari and distanced him from the intellectual freedom that was central to Muʿtazilism – a philosophy that naturally gave rise to revolutionary social movements.

The second factor was subjective, linked to al-Ashʿari's intellectual limitations in dealing with ideological and philosophical questions, which led him to surrender to religious mysticism. He became convinced that reason was too weak to grasp divine truths and that such truths were subject to faith. This conviction distanced him from Muʿtazilism, which held that reason could resolve religious problems.

Despite this, al-Ashʿari employed logical argumentation in his battle against Muʿtazilism and sought to reconcile reason with the Sunna. However, when faced with intellectual dead-ends, he ultimately resorted to the Quran, the Sunna, and the accounts of the Prophet's companions, as well as the works of prominent Imams of Hadith.

3 The Social Principles of Ashʿarism

The Ashʿarite school of thought emerged as a comprehensive ideological framework through philosophical engagement with Muʿtazilism. One of the central debates between the two schools concerned the attributes of God and His role in the universe. Contrary to the Muʿtazilites' rejection of anthropomorphic descriptions of God, the Ashʿarites interpreted Quranic verses such as 'And there will remain the Face of your Lord, Owner of Majesty and Honor' (Quran 55:27) and '… both His hands are extended …' (Quran 5:64) in a very literal way.

Although al-Ashʿari had, under Muʿtazilite influence, initially supported the idea of human free will, he later declared that 'God creates humans and all their deeds, whether good or evil, immoral or seductive, obedient or spiritually guided',[27] rejecting the Muʿtazilite embrace of *qadariyya* (absolute freedom of choice), and arguing that God's purpose is ultimately goodness and justice.

Ashʿarism's social outlook was most evident in two key areas: the Caliphate (or governance) and the nature of the Holy Quran. Regarding the Caliphate, al-Ashʿari asserted that it should belong to Quraysh, opposing the Kharijites, who argued it should go to the most pious individual, regardless of lineage. He

27 Al-Shmali n.d., p. 210.

also opposed *al-ansar* (the Prophet's supporters from Medina), *ahl al-bayt* (the Prophet's family), and the Umayyads, supporting the Abbasids in their struggle against the Shiʿites, particularly the Fatimids, who established a rival Caliphate in Egypt.

In the theological realm, al-Ashʿari rejected the Muʿtazilite doctrine of the Quran's createdness, maintaining instead that the Quran is eternal. Despite this apparent glorification, the Ashʿarites, in alignment with the ruling authorities, declared that 'the Sunnah transcends the Quran, while the Quran does not transcend the Sunnah'.[28] This was based on verses such as: 'O Messenger, announce that which has been revealed to you from your Lord' (Quran 5:67) and '… Whatever the Messenger has given you – take; and what he has forbidden you – refrain from' (Quran 69:7). They argued that since the Prophet served as the intermediary for divine revelation, it would be illogical for him to contradict the message.

Considering that the Hadith was not documented during the Prophet's lifetime but rather after his death – a fact that remains highly controversial due to the introduction of additional content – it is likely that various factions selectively cited specific Hadiths to justify their positions and actions. In this regard, the political regression of Ashʿarism is particularly notable, especially as articulated by al-Ghazali (Muhammad al-Ghazali, also known as Abu Hamid and nicknamed Hujjat al-Islam, 450–505 AH/1058–1111 CE). Al-Ghazali posed the question: 'What should be done if a ruler lacks the competence to lead, but consults with religious scholars? He may be deposed and replaced, provided that such an action does not incite conflict or *fitna* (civil strife). However, if deposing him would lead to disorder, he should be obeyed, and his imamate maintained'.[29] This reasoning suggests that enduring corrupt or incompetent rulers is preferable to the instability caused by popular revolutions (20). One of al-Ghazali's contemporaries, Aʿmaq,[30] similarly endorsed tyranny, arguing that it was better than the chaos that would result from revolutionary upheaval.[31]

The most concerning aspect of Ashʿarite thought was their denial of the existence of any 'scientific law', thereby rejecting the idea of a consistent natural order underlying all phenomena. This denial opened the door for the promotion of miracles, effectively negating humanity's role in shaping historical developments.

---

28 Yahia ibn Kathir, cited in Grunebaum 1956, p. 143.

29 Grunebaum 1956, 217.

30 Aʿmaq, was a contemporary thinker of Al-Ghazali.

31 Grunebaum 1956, 450.

While it has been noted that the triumph of Ashʿarism represented a significant intellectual regression, this is not the whole truth. This shift stifled research and inquiry, constraining intellectual freedom with rigid doctrinal limitations. As a result, thinkers like Ibn Khaldun were unable to exercise serene and reasonable judgment fully. In his *Muqaddimah* (Prolegomena), Ibn Khaldun harshly criticised Muʿtazilism, deeming its schools of thought corrupt, and advocating instead for inner faith and reliance on personal convictions. He was a strong supporter of Abu Hasan al-Ashʿari and sought to shut down any further theological debate, asserting that 'scholastic study of Islamic theology is no longer necessary for knowledge seekers today. It was important in earlier times to refute blasphemy, which has since faded away, and Sunni Imams have provided sufficient explanations through their writings'.[32]

Understanding this historical context in both its backward- and forward-looking dimensions helps clarify the truth. Ibn Khaldun, who approached history from a materialist perspective and analyzed the economic motivations behind historical development, ultimately critiqued Ashʿarism, despite his defense of its ideas. His analysis addressed the prevailing intellectual climate of his era, particularly in relation to the decline of Muʿtazilism, and remained relevant up until the Renaissance.

32 Complete bibliographic details not provided in Tuma's original citation. (A.K.)

CHAPTER 7

Al- Shuʿubiyya: An Ideology of Equality and National Fanaticism

Writers and historians from various eras of the Islamic Arab Empire, often influenced by their social classes – primarily ideologically rather than economically – distorted the image of progressive movements and ideas to protect and defend the ruling authorities. Those who followed continued this pattern. However, in recent years, an enlightened progressive movement has emerged, aiming to liberate these progressive ideas from the falsifications and misrepresentations imposed upon them. This movement seeks to restore these ideas to their rightful place in the history of Arab societies, whether in their socioeconomic foundations or ideological superstructures.

Among the ideological currents subjected to various distortions was *Shuʿubiyya*, which has been particularly targeted by contemporary Arab reactionaries to attack communism and undermine its positive attributes. By the late 1960s, *Shuʿubiyya* became synonymous with communism in the political rhetoric of Arab reactionaries. Those labeled as 'Shuʿubiyyūn' were accused of 'national nihilism' and rejecting Arabism. Ironically, those inciting the Arab masses against communism were often the least knowledgeable about the true nature and historical development of 'Shuʿubiyya', revealing their ignorance on the subject.

This raises fundamental questions: What, in fact, was *Shuʿubiyya*? When did it emerge? And in which direction did it develop?

1 A Disposition, a Phenomenon, or an Intellectual Current?

Given the difficulty of defining the precise nature of *Shuʿubiyya* – or more accurately, given the multiplicity of its manifestations – some historians and writers have tended to regard it as a mere *disposition*. In their view, it was neither a movement around which broad masses rallied and interacted with historical events at a given stage, nor a fully articulated intellectual system that could be situated within the ideological superstructure and categorised as such. Rather, they argue, it was an inclination or a mental attitude – an intellectual tendency that expressed a particular stance and embodied a certain state of mind.

 | HTTPS://DOI.ORG/10.1163/9789004774261-012

Others, favouring simplification and generalisation, have described *Shuʿubiyya* as a socio-political *phenomenon* that crystallised in the enumeration of Arab shortcomings. Its clearest expression, they contend, was to be found in literature. Yet such generalisations may be somewhat unjust to those historians who sought to evaluate it more objectively, thereby exposing certain of its genuine features.

2 Objective Opinions

In his *History of Islamic Civilization* (*Tarikh al-Tamaddun al-Islami*), Jurji Zaydan notes that *Shuʿubiyya* manifested itself in attacks against the Arabs during the reign of the Abbasid caliph al-Ma'mun and his successors.[1] He adds that al-Ma'mun favored certain *Shuʿubis* who openly disparaged the Arabs, such as Sahl ibn Harun, Abu ʿUbayda al-Rawiya, and ʿAllan al-Shuʿubi. Zaydan further records that the *Shuʿubis* upheld the principle of equality, citing prophetic traditions such as: 'Muslims are brothers; their blood is of equal worth; their protection extends even to the least of them; and they stand united against others'. They also referred to the Prophet's Farewell Sermon: 'No Arab has superiority over a non-Arab except by piety'.

Philip Hitti, in his *History of the Arabs*, concurs with Zaydan.[2] He writes: 'Its essence [i.e., Shuʿubiyya] was the call for equality among all Muslims. And although it was expressed among the Kharijites and the Shiʿa, and in some Persian circles took on a religious coloration – such as *zandaqa* and related tendencies – it generally assumed the form of literary polemics, ridiculing the Arabs' claims of intellectual superiority and asserting instead that excellence in poetry and literature belonged to non-Arabs'.[3]

Gustav von Grunebaum likewise did not deviate from this assessment. In his *Medieval Islam*, he regarded the Shuʿubiyya as a movement initially aimed at political equality that later shifted into the realm of scholarly and literary disputation. He explained:

> The name of this intellectual and cultural movement, the 'Shuʿubiyya', derives from a Quranic verse that tells believers: 'O mankind, indeed We have created you from male and female and made you peoples [Shuʿub] and tribes that you may know one another. Indeed, the most noble of you in the sight of Allah is

1 Zaydan 1922, pp. 144–45.
2 Hitti 1952, p. 488.
3 Ibid.

> the most righteous of you. Indeed, Allah is Knowing and Acquainted' (Q 49:13). This verse, he notes, was interpreted as a command to achieve equality not only among Arab tribes but also between Arabs and the non-Arab Shuʿub (peoples).[4]

According to *al-ʿIqd al-Farid* (the unique necklace), Ahmad Amin, in his book *Duha al-Islam* discusses al-Shuʿubiyya, writing that 'it argues that the Arabs are not superior to other nations, as no nation is inherently better than another; all people are equal'. He emphasises that distinctions should be made between individuals, not between nations:

> people are not distinguished by their origins or ancestors, but by their deeds, morals, dignity, and strong will and diligence. A person lacking in strong will and morals will not be worthy of respect or honor, even if he descends from the noblest tribes and origins. True honor and generosity come from noble acts and strong will, not from family lineage or ancestry.[5]

3 Al-Shuʿubiyya as a Reaction to the Political Failures of the Ruling Authority

From all this, it becomes clear that the Shuʿubiyya emerged as a call for equality among the diverse peoples of the Islamic empire. Within this framework, it represented a response to the contradiction between the foundational principles of Islam – which emphasised equality among Muslims regardless of ethnic, tribal, or familial affiliation – and the political reality of the empire, which privileged Arabs, particularly the Qurashis, by elevating them to positions of authority in the expanding polity.

We would not agree, however, with Philip Hitti's assessment that the Shuʿubiyya, understood as a doctrine of 'egalitarianism', was fully embodied in the principles of the Kharijites and the Shiʿa.[6] Yet it is possible to acknowledge that the Kharijite rejection of Qurashi or Arab exclusivity in the caliphate was consistent with Islam's declared message of equality, and may indeed have contributed – directly or indirectly – to the later development of Shuʿubi thought.[7]

4 Grunebaum 1956, p. 123.
5 Amin 1933, p. 52.
6 Hitti 1970, pp. 307–9. Hitti interprets Kharijite and Shiʿi opposition to Qurashi dominance as an early manifestation of egalitarianism akin to Shuʿubiyya. (A.K.)
7 On the Kharijite conception of the caliphate and its resonance with broader egalitarian ideals, see Crone 2004, pp. 54–63.

Although Shiʿism represented a progressive current in Islam during both the Umayyad and Abbasid caliphates, its insistence on the exclusive right of the ʿAlids (referring to Ali ibn Abi Talib and his descendants) to the Caliphate and the Imamate was a significant factor in its relative setback in political and religious leadership compared to the Kharijites and Muʿtazilites. The Muʿtazilites, as exemplified by Dirar ibn ʿAmr,[8] argued that non-Arabs, 'even Nabataeans', were more deserving of leadership than the Quraysh, as they could be more easily deposed if proven to be tyrannical (Ibid, p. 60).

Within this context, Ash-Shuʿubiyya initially emerged as a continuation of progressive currents advocating for equality among the various peoples of the Islamic community. It arose in response to the ruling authority's failure to uphold this equality in line with clear Islamic teachings, instead favoring political practices that, from the day of the Prophet's death and the selection of the first Caliph, Abu Bakr, distinguished Arabs in general and the Quraysh in particular.

4 When did Ash-Shuʿubiyya Emerge?

There is no conclusive evidence that the *Shuʿubiyya* movement arose during the Umayyad caliphate. The participation of the Persians in the ʿAbbasid *daʿwa*, which was initially based in Khurasan, was not inspired by *Shuʿubiyya* or by an egalitarian program. Rather, it reflected two interrelated factors: first, resentment against Umayyad political domination, which had struck heavy blows against the Persian landed elites and, as a class-based regime, had served as an instrument of exploitation and repression; and second, the expression of national sentiment rooted in attachment to the pre-Islamic imperial past and the grandeur of the Sasanian Empire.

While it is difficult to precisely determine the extent of nationalist fervor during this period of political upheaval, it is clear that such sentiments were present. Ibrahim al-Imam, a Persian leader, reportedly wrote to Abu Muslim al-Khurasani, the military leader of the Abbasid *daʿwa*, saying:

---

8 Dirar ibn ʿAmr (d. ca. 800 CE) was an early Muslim theologian associated with the formative period of the Muʿtazila. Though not among its "five principles" formulators, he is considered one of its important predecessors, often described as a *mutaqaddim* (forerunner). His teachings emphasised divine justice, the createdness of the Quran, and political accountability of rulers, and he is reported to have argued that a just non-Arab ruler could be preferable to an unjust Qurashi.

> If you could kill whoever speaks Arabic in Khorasan, do so! And if you doubt the loyalty of any child or boy whose height reaches five spans, kill him, especially if he is a son of Mudhar (the largest Arab tribe), as they are the most threatening enemy. Eradicate them entirely – humans and property.[9]

Given this context, it is difficult to pinpoint the exact period in which al-Shuʿubiyya emerged, particularly as the information transmitted directly by Shuʿubi proponents is scarce and lacks concrete evidence. Ahmad Amin suggests that the loss of Shuʿubi texts is due to the fact that 'Muslims considered Aa-Shuʿubiyya hostile to Islam; therefore, they refrained from preserving books written about it. Some even sought to gain favor with God by destroying these works, thus protecting believers from being influenced by it'. Al-Zamakhshari[10] echoed this sentiment in the introduction of his book *Al-Mufassal*, where he thanked God 'for making him proud of Arabism, for defending the Arabs and their history, and for saving him from joining the Shuʿubis'.[11]

It is likely, therefore, that the *Shuʿubiyya* movement emerged after the establishment of the ʿAbbasid state and before the fall of the Barmakids, the ministers of Caliph Harun al-Rashid.

5 Shuʿubiyya or Shuʿubiyyas?

Ibn Qutayba,[12] one of the most ardent partisans of the Arabs and the author of *Tafdil al-ʿArab* (Favoring the Arabs), claimed that those who adopted al-Shuʿubiyya were largely from the lower classes. He wrote:

> I have not seen among the Shuʿubiyya any who harbor deeper enmity or greater hostility toward the Arabs than the rabble, the riffraff, the ignoble Nabateans, and

---

9 Amin n.d., p. 32.

10 Al-Zamakhsharī (1075–1144 CE), Persian scholar and Qur'anic exegete, known for his linguistic and theological commentary *Al-Kashshaf* and his association with the Muʿtazilite tradition.

11 Amin n.d., p. 70.

12 Ibn Qutaybah (Abu Muhammad ʿAbd Allah ibn Muslim al-Dinawari, d. 276 AH / 889 CE) was a prominent Arab philologist, jurist, and historian of Persian descent. He served as a qadi (judge) in Dinawar and was closely associated with the Abbasid court in Baghdad. His works, such as *ʿUyun al-Akhbar*, *Kitab al-Maʿarif*, and *Tafdil al-ʿArab*, reflect his defence of Arab cultural primacy and opposition to the Shuʿubiyya movement, making him a central figure in the intellectual debates over Arab versus non-Arab identity in early Abbasid society.

> the sons of the most despicable villages. As for the noble Persians, their men of rank, and those devoted to religion, they know both their rights and their obligations and recognize lineage as a fixed source of honour.[13]

This image reflects the nature of popular Shuʿubiyya in its early stages, as a movement representing specific social classes that sought to achieve equality and end nationalist oppression and discrimination. In this context, al-Shuʿubiyya spread among various groups within the Islamic Arab Empire, with its form and representation differing in each province, according to the conditions of the province and its residents. For example, al-Shuʿubiyya among the Nabataeans (the Aramaic-speaking peasants of Upper Mesopotamia) was expressed through an emphasis on land and agriculture, favouring farming and cultivation over the nomadic desert lifestyle.[14] In other words, the struggle manifested as a fight for land and the right to agricultural practices, in response to the authority's attempts to suppress them by confiscating their lands or depriving them of the ability to farm.

Gustave von Grunebaum gave particular attention to the Shuʿubiyya of the Zanj, who occupied the lowest rung of the social hierarchy. He wrote: 'History, with the passage of time, secured equality between the Persian and the Arab (!) and between the Turk and the Arab (!), yet it did not assist the Black Muslim in defending his racial right'. As a result, a specifically Zanji Shuʿubiyya emerged, one of whose rhetorical themes was the emphasis on Abyssinia's role in hosting the first Muslim emigrants. Nevertheless, the Zanj did not contribute extensively to Shuʿubiyya as a literary movement; rather, they played a far more decisive role as they constituted the principal contingent of the slave army in the great social uprising known as the 'Zanj Rebellion' of the third AH /ninth CE century.

Like other sociopolitical movements, Shuʿubiyya was associated by contemporary writers, particularly those who supported the class system, with heresy, in order to undermine its call for equality within the Islamic Arab Empire. In this regard, we can see that Ibn Qutayba was correct, from his class-based perspective, when he argued that the class composition of Shuʿubiyya in its early days – focused on achieving equality – was shaped by the 'rabble' (*al-safala*) and the 'riffraff' (*al-awbash,*) a portrayal that reflects how the upper classes have often depicted popular movements throughout history.

---

13 Amin n.d., p. 62.

14 Amin n.d., p. 59.

In this Abbasid period, class polarisation was particularly acute, transcending ethnic boundaries and uniting the upper strata around their shared interests on the one hand, while on the other uniting the dispossessed masses of the various peoples. This dynamic was explicitly articulated by Caliph al-Ma'mun, who declared: 'Nobility lies in lineage: a noble Arab has more claim to a noble Persian than a base-born Persian has to his own nobleman; and a noble Persian has more claim to a noble Arab than a base-born Arab has to his own nobleman'.[15]

It is difficult to determine precisely when *Shuʿubiyya* shifted from a position of advocating equality to one of ethnic chauvinism, and from a progressive intellectual current to a reactionary one. What is clear, however, is that the Abbasid Caliphate's decline unfolded in stages, during which the very nature of *Shuʿubiyya* changed. It came to represent an ideology of ethnic superiority and a discourse aimed at denigrating the Arabs, who were regarded as the dominant ruling group.

This development should not be seen as a form of modern-style 'national awakening', such as that witnessed during humanity's struggles against imperialism and colonialism. The issue was not marked by comparable intensity, nor was the divide between the upper classes of different ethnic groups particularly deep or sharply defined. In this regard, Ahmad Amin observed that the Abbasid caliphs were zealous for Islam but not for Arab ethnicity. From this, it becomes clear that the Abbasid caliphs who came to power with Persian support did not suppress *Shuʿubiyya* in its later phase, when it became an expression of primarily Persian ethnic chauvinism; rather, they tolerated and even encouraged it.

Within this framework, we could view Shuʿubiyya in its second phase as a chauvinistic nationalist ideological current that became part of the ideology of the non-Arab rulers. The foundation for this shift was laid by the founder of the Abbasid Caliphate, who appealed to the people of Khurasan for support, saying: 'O people of Khurasan, you are our supporters and advocates, and the disseminators of our cause'.[16] Before his death, al-Mansur advised his son, saying:

> I instruct you to be kind to the people of Khurasan, for they are your supporters and advocates, who gave their money and sacrificed their blood for your state. Do not let your love depart from their hearts; treat them well, overlook their mistakes, reward those who deserve it, and take care of the children and families of the deceased.[17] (*At-Tabari*, Vol. 9, p. 219).

15 Al-Thaʿalibi n.d., p. 219.
16 Al-Tabari 1987, vol. 9, p. 127.
17 Al-Tabari 1987, vol. 9, 219.

While Harun al-Rashid restored some balance between Arab and non-Arab (Persian) influence through his suppression of the Barmakids, the struggle between al-Amin and al-Ma'mun took on the form of a contest between Arabs and Persians. Al-Ma'mun's victory marked the triumph of Persian influence. In this context, al-Tabari recorded:

> A man thrust himself forward on several occasions before al-Ma'mun when the latter was in Syria and said to the Caliph, 'O Commander of the Faithful, look after the interests of the Arabs of Syria just as you look after the interests of the Persians from the people of Khurasan'. Al-Ma'mun replied, 'O brother from the people of Syria, you have reproached me in strong terms! By God, I have never made Qays dismount from the backs of their horses [that is, dismissed them from service] except at times when I saw that there was not a single dirham left in the public treasury [in times of great financial stringency]. As for Yaman, I have never liked them and they have never liked me. As for Qudaʿah, their chiefs live in the messianic expectation of al-Sufyani[18] and his appearance, so that they might join his party. As for Rabiʿah, they have been angry with God ever since He sent His prophet from Mudar.'[19]

It is no coincidence that a poet of Al-Mutawakkil's court would later chant similar sentiments, reflecting the growing division between Arab and Persian factions within the Abbasid empire:

> I am proud, the son of noble Jamshid's line,[20]
> The heir to the kings of Persia.
> I will restore the glory of my ancestors,
> Their greatness lost long ago.
>
> With the knowledge of the Kayanians,[21]
> I claim the right to lead the nations.
> Tell Banu Hashim to surrender,
> Before regret finds them too late.

---

18 Al-Sufyani refers to a prophetic figure in Islamic eschatology, particularly in Shia tradition, who is expected to appear as a tyrant from Syria before the end times, opposed to the Mahdi, and whose emergence is considered one of the signs preceding the Day of Judgment. (A.K.)

19 Al-Tabari 1987, vol. 32, pp. 233–4.

20 Reference to King Jamshid of Persia.

21 Kaveh, is a legendary blacksmith hero in Persian mythology and the *Shahnameh*, who led a popular revolt against the tyrant king Zahhak (Dahak).

We conquered you with spears,
Subdued you with swords.
Return to your lands in the Hijaz,
To your herds and the simple life of nomads.

I will take the throne of kings,
With the sword in hand and knowledge at my side.

This nationalist, chauvinistic Shuʿubi current found overt expression in literature, often descending into futile and racist arguments that sometimes reached the level of vulgarity. However, this mutual vulgarity did not entirely obscure the initial tendency toward reconciliation that characterised the early stages of Shuʿubiyya. For instance, despite the Persian poet al-Khuraymi's pride in his Persian ancestry and his disdain for Arabs, he still celebrated his people with a spirit that reflected this tension, chanting: 'True pride comes not from appearances or titles, but from virtue and wisdom. Laws govern everyone equally, and in death, all are the same'.

This verse philosophically embodies the principle of equality among people, and even Ibn Qutayba, who strongly supported the Arabs and placed them above other nations, acknowledged in his book *Tafdil al-ʿArab*:

> I reasonably argue that all people come from the same origins, as all humans descend from our first father and mother. All humans were created from dust, and they will return to dust. Like all creatures, humans are subject to the laws of nature, and their lives are inevitably determined by destiny. This should deter wise minds from self-glorification, arrogance, and pride in ancestry or social class, for all such distinctions are nullified at the moment of death, except for a person's piety and obedience to God.

In fact, the Shuʿubiyya, in both their reactionary and progressive phases, never opposed Islam. Shuʿubi thinkers who favoured the Persians often cited Hadiths attributed to the Prophet that, although seemingly superficial, emphasised the superiority of Persians and warned against mistreating them, such as: 'Do not curse the Persians, and whoever does so will face consequences sooner or later'. This was a counter to Arab chauvinists, who frequently cited Hadiths suggesting Arab superiority, such as: 'I will never mediate for those who deceive the Arabs, nor will I be kind', or 'if people disagree, Banu Mudar[22] will always be right'.

---

22 Banu Mudar was one of the major tribal groups of northern Arabia (Adnanite Arabs), trad-

The question that arises here is: To what extent did Shuʿubiyya influence Islamic-Arab thought and sociopolitical movements? Based on the aforementioned information, we can draw two conclusions:

- Shuʿubiyya played a role in diminishing Arab nationalist chauvinism and racist arrogance.
- Shuʿubiyya laid the groundwork for the emergence of revolutionary progressive movements, though it did not constitute an essential part of the ideologies of movements like the Qarmatians, the Zanj, and others.

itionally considered descendants of Mudar ibn Nizar, including prominent tribes such as Quraysh, Tamim, and Qays, who played crucial roles in pre-Islamic Arabia and the early Islamic conquests. (A.K.)

CHAPTER 8

The Relationship between Religion and Nationalism

1 Historical Aspects

Reading certain historical works gives a mistaken impression about the relationship between religion and nationalism, as they suggest that humanity passed through two distinct stages: one dominated by religion, and a later stage where it regressed in favour of emerging nationalism. However, reality differs from this idealistic and mechanistic view, as religion and nationalism have interacted throughout history, and this interaction continues to the present day. Therefore, it is important to define this relationship within the framework of social transitions from one era to another, where the real equation becomes clear to everyone.

Without delving deeply into the specific motives behind the emergence of religion or its social roles, it can be argued that religion has historically served as a crucial intellectual factor in fostering social bonds – whether among members of the same tribe or between different tribes. Religion shaped the relationships within tribes, playing a foundational role in maintaining social cohesion. It is no coincidence that religion was seen as the superstructure reflecting the economic base and social relations during the production of the means of life.

As tribes transitioned from pastoral economies to agricultural ones, and the first kingdoms arose in the Nile Basin (Egypt), Mesopotamia (Iraq), the Yellow River (China), the Ganges (India), and elsewhere, religion took on a central role in the ruling institutions. It became a fundamental pillar of monarchies, reinforcing the myth that kings and pharaohs were descended from gods. In this way, monarchs occupied the pinnacle of the social hierarchy, encompassing all economic and political levels. Consequently, gods were inherently class-based, legitimising exploitation and slavery. In this ancient historical context, it was possible to speak of races, lineages, and ethnic origins, since intermixing among diverse tribes and developing peoples was still nascent. From this perspective, myths of human origins arose: the Greeks traced themselves to their ancestor Hēlas, the Hebrews preserved Abraham as their forefather, and the Arabs claimed descent from Isma'il.

As primitive nationalist sentiments emerged, the unity of origin remained strong, and religion occupied the centre of social cohesion. Early historians

 | HTTPS://DOI.ORG/10.1163/9789004774261-013

like Herodotus note that the Athenians once mobilised based on 'blood kinship among all Greeks, the unity of language, temples, common sacrifices, and similarity of lifestyle'.[1]

The Roman Empire represents the culmination of early human development in the relationship between religion and primitive nationalism. Roman emperors deified themselves and imposed their worship upon subjugated peoples, sparking conflict. Although the uprisings that erupted were primarily driven by economic factors – such as the burdens of taxation, the exploitation of workers, and the plundering of national resources – they often carried religious banners. The Revolt of the jews in Palestine in 70 CE provides a clear example of this.

However, it would be wrong to overstate religion's ability to mobilise the masses against Caesars. The most significant Roman-era uprising was the slave revolt led by Spartacus, which was non-religious and non-nationalist, highlighting the decisive role of class struggle: people of various ethnic backgrounds united against slavery.

The truth is that the triumph of Christianity, despite the brutal persecution by the Roman Empire, was due to its social message, which resonated with the foundations of the Christian faith. The submission to a heavenly Father, the belief that His son, Jesus Christ, was crucified to save humanity from its original sin, and the promise of an Afterlife in Paradise, aligned with the hopes of the masses in the Roman Empire. These masses, burdened by class struggles and regional uprisings, had fallen to the lowest rungs of society, further exacerbating the suffering of the poor, whether free or enslaved.

The spread of Christianity throughout Europe laid the groundwork for the Papacy to combine both religious and worldly authority. While it succeeded to some extent in expanding its influence across Western Christendom, it faced resistance from kings and princes who sought to preserve their class-based interests and were reluctant to share power with the clergy. Nevertheless, the papacy, which dominated Western and Central Europe, reflected in its religious ideology the feudal fragmentation that accompanied the rise of Catholicism. With the emergence of modern nationalism, however, the authority of the papacy declined, and its capacity to employ religion as a means of curbing the power of princes and kings was significantly diminished.

Undoubtedly, Catholicism, under the leadership of the papal institution and its extensive apparatus, was able to transcend to a considerable degree

1 Complete bibliographic details not provided in Tuma's original citation. (A.K.)

the primordial expressions of national sentiment. Yet, it could not ultimately block their emergence or suppress their development. In fact, the waves of rebellion against Catholicism often took the form of religious reforms with a distinctly nationalist character. In this regard, Protestantism represented a dual revolution: a religious uprising combined with nationalist resentment, tied to specific regions. This blend of nationalist and religious motivations was clearly demonstrated in the reforms of Jan Hus,[2] the Czech theologian and church reformer. Perhaps nothing illustrates the dual nature of the Hussite cause more vividly than the proclamation issued by its leaders following their military victory at the Battle of Vyšehrad on 5 November 1420, which declared:

> We appeal to you, out of love and compassion, to have mercy on yourselves and on your people and to cooperate with us in order to save the Divine Law from the persecution planned by the Monarch and his minions. He wants to deprive us of salvation by imposing his heretic school upon us, leading us to hell. But if you, despite this, choose to side with the monarch, we will conclude that you are the reason behind the disappearance of the Bohemian nation, and will treat you, according to God's will, as enemies of God and the nation.[3]

When Martin Luther launched his campaign against papal authority and the indulgences that were sold for money, he called for the purification of Christianity from the accumulated superstitions of clerical mediation between humankind and God. His message quickly resonated with German princes and knights, particularly through his celebrated pamphlet *An Appeal to the German Nobility*. In this spirit, Luther and his allies, the German knights led by Ulrich von Hutten,[4] became active during the first quarter of the sixteenth century.[5]

---

2 Jan Hus (c. 1372–1415) was a Czech priest, theologian, and reformer. He became known for criticising clerical corruption and the sale of indulgences, advocating instead for the authority of Scripture and moral reform within the Church. Condemned as a heretic, he was burned at the stake at the Council of Constance in 1415. His death inspired the Hussite movement in Bohemia, which combined religious reform with elements of Czech national consciousness. (A.K.)

3 Quoted in Baron 1947, p. 11.

4 Ulrich von Hutten (1488–1523) was a German knight, humanist, and poet who became a fervent supporter of Martin Luther and the Reformation. He is remembered for his satirical writings against the papacy and his role in linking humanist ideals with the nationalist and reformist aspirations of the early sixteenth century.

5 Robinson 1926, pp. 288–96.

Historians generally maintain that the reforms proposed by Luther combined both religious and social concerns, constituting the intellectual framework of the nascent bourgeoisie that was emerging within the womb of a decaying feudal economy and, albeit without full clarity at the time, aimed at overcoming feudal fragmentation.

The break of England's King Henry VIII (r. 1509–47) from the Papacy in 1533 was not solely due to the Pope's refusal to annul his marriage to Catherine of Aragon, sister of the Spanish princes and aunt of Emperor Charles V. Rather, it reflected the English ruling class's desire to free itself from foreign religious domination and establish a national church that represented growing nationalist sentiments. King Henry VIII succeeded in securing the support of the English clergy to establish the Church of England (Anglican Church), and in 1533, Parliament confirmed that his marriage to Catherine was illegal, declaring the king 'the only supreme head on earth of the Church of England'.[6]

We can assert that the weakening of the universal Catholic Church in the fifteenth and sixteenth centuries, following the spread of religious reformist movements – despite their varying currents – within Protestantism and the dissolution of feudalism, prevented religion from being used as a banner for colonialism and later Imperialism as Europe began occupying lands in Asia and Africa. While the universal papal church succeeded in rallying princes, knights, and kings to declare crusades in the eleventh and twelfth centuries to occupy the Holy Land and neighbouring regions in the Near East, from the seventeenth century onward, colonists and imperialists felt compelled to justify their conquests under the banner of national pride and the 'civilising' of so-called barbarian peoples.

However, this does not change the fundamental economic drivers of both stages. The Crusades aimed to alleviate the crisis of feudalism in Europe on the one hand and to serve the economic interests of Italian city-states on the other. In contrast, colonial wars sought to plunder African and Asian resources, marking the beginning of the financial accumulation that preceded capitalism and accelerating the process of capitalist development.

The emergence of Islam provides a classic example of the organic connection between religion and primal nationalism. Through his religious and worldly mission, Prophet Muhammad sought to unite all Arab tribes into one nation. He integrated social reforms with the enhancement of nationalist sentiments, while simultaneously transcending Arab nationalism by extending his

6 Robinson 1926, p. 317.

message to all nations, making Islam a universal standard for evaluating human worth, as captured in his famous statement: 'an Arab has no superiority over a non-Arab ... except by piety and good action'.

Among the three monotheistic religions – Judaism, Christianity, and Islam – no other faith so deeply integrated religious and worldly matters as Islam did. This is symbolically reflected in the title given to the caliphs who followed the Prophet, 'Commanders of the Faithful'. Yet, this fusion of religion and worldly governance did not prevent various social and national movements from rebelling against the Caliphate when they disagreed with its stance on either religious or worldly matters.

We believe that the Azhari scholar, ʿAli ʿAbdel Raziq,[7] was not far from the truth in his book *Islam and the Foundations of Governance* when he argued that the state established in early Islam was an Arab state, built upon the foundations of the religious *daʿwa*, upholding the banner of defending this *daʿwa* and relying upon it. He also noted that Muslims at that time understood they were establishing a civil, secular state. Therefore, they rebelled against it, knowing their dispute was about worldly matters and not religious issues (though there were also religious disagreements, as the case of the Shiʿites illustrates, although socioeconomic factors also influenced their opposition). Raziq further contended that their disagreement was over political matters that did not affect their religion or destabilise their faith (published in Cairo, 1925, p. 94).[8]

The strong connection between religious and worldly matters in Islam is evident in the fact that all major social and political movements – the rebellion against Uthman, the Zanj Rebellion, and the Qarmatian Rebellion – were waged under religious banners. Their ideological framework was based on Islamic jurisprudential concepts that conflicted with those of the ruling authority. What is significant in this context is that, despite Islam's universal inclusiveness and its transcendence of national divisions among its adherents, it did not prevent national conflicts. The Shuʿubi movement, though also driven by socioeconomic motives, expressed a struggle for equality between people and, in its later stages, became a manifestation of supremacist chauvinism.

7 ʿAli ʿAbd al-Raziq (1888–1966) was an Egyptian Islamic scholar and jurist, best known for his controversial work *Islam and the Foundations of Governance* (1925), in which he argued that the early Islamic state was fundamentally political and not inherently religious, separating the authority of the caliphate from divine mandate.

8 ʿAli ʿAbd al-Raziq, *al-Islam w-Usul al-Hokm* [Islam and the Foundations of Governance] (Cairo: Dar al-Hilal, 1925), 94.

2 The Emergence of Contemporary Nationalist Movements

So far, we have used the term 'nationalist' in reference to the nationalist sentiments that motivated oppressed nations to resist foreign tyranny. However, we do not claim that the feudal era gave birth to contemporary nationalist movements. Rather, these movements emerged within the specific historical circumstances that contributed to the rise of the bourgeoisie and its struggle to overcome feudal fragmentation and sectarian divisions.

This is why, when religious reforms were linked with nationalist ideas, as we saw in Bohemia, England, and the German principalities, the nationalist vision was neither comprehensive nor profound. It is not surprising, therefore, that some German principalities remained Catholic until the very end. In Anglican Britain, Catholics did not feel loyalty to the Anglican monarchy but instead to the Catholic Church. They even cooperated with Catholic kings who conspired against the ruling authority under the banner of defending Catholicism and seeking its triumph.

As a result, the Catholic Church actively opposed nationalism during the period when nationalist movements were emerging in Europe, viewing it as blasphemy and misguidance. For example, the Synod[9] of Vienna in 1849, which was composed of thirty-five bishops, expressed gratitude to Emperor Franz Joseph of Austria (1830–1916), stating that he had 'received from God his noble mission to manage, strengthen, and unite all the nations comprising the empire'. The synod also condemned nationalist principles, declaring that the linguistic differences upon which nationalism is based stemmed from 'disobedience and misguidance', serving as 'clear evidence of the Creator's anger'.[10]

It was evident that the clergy in the Austro-Hungarian Empire, through this decision, sought to bolster the imperial authority, which was facing turbulent nationalist revolutions in 1848. The most significant of these was the Hungarian Revolution, where the Hungarian people sought to establish an independent nation-state. This revolution, along with other nationalist movements that erupted during the revolutionary wave of 1848, signalled the decline of religious dominance, though not its complete elimination, as nationalist concepts took centre stage and played a decisive role in shaping events.

9 The term *synod* refers to an ecclesiastical council within the Christian tradition, usually convened by bishops to deliberate on doctrinal, disciplinary, or administrative matters of the Church. In Catholic usage, synods often served to affirm orthodoxy and respond to political or theological challenges. (A.K.)

10 Quoted in al-Husari 1963, p. 23.

During this historical period, marked by the rise of the bourgeois system, sectarian structures and barriers began to collapse on both national and international levels, giving way to the idea of nationalism and its associated popular movements. In the early phase of bourgeois ascendancy, as Lenin observed, feudalism and absolutism fell apart, leading to the emergence of a bourgeois-democratic society and state. This was the first time that national movements became mass movements, engaging all social classes in politics through various means such as the press and participation in representative institutions.[11]

The collapse of feudalism and absolute monarchy, along with the political involvement of all social classes, marked the beginning of the end of sectarianism and the beginning of the separation of church and state. The French Revolution, the quintessential bourgeois revolution in Europe at the close of the seventeenth century, exemplifies the establishment of a democratic bourgeois state that abolished sectarian divisions, ensured equality for Protestants and French Jews, and firmly separated church from state.

In the nineteenth century, amid the rise of a turbulent nationalist wave, the German principalities were unified into the German Empire, despite the religious divide between Catholics and Protestants. Similarly, the Italian provinces were unified through battles against foreign rule, particularly the Austro-Hungarian Empire, as well as against feudal reactionaries and the Papacy, which sought to maintain both its secular authority and concrete dominance in certain regions.

Undoubtedly, language, along with other factors, played a critical role in determining the territorial borders within which nation-states established their authority. This was affirmed by Lenin, who wrote:

> Throughout the world, the period of the final victory of capitalism over feudalism has been linked up with national movements. For the complete victory of commodity production, the bourgeoisie must capture the home market, and there must be politically united territories whose population speak a single language, with all obstacles to the development of that language and to its consolidation in literature eliminated. Therein is the economic foundation of national movements. Language is the most important means of human intercourse. Unity and unimpeded development of language are the most important conditions for genuinely free and extensive commerce on a scale commensurate with modern capitalism.[12]

11 Lenin 1914.
12 Lenin 1914.

Yet, religious zealots reject the material facts surrounding the nature of nationalist movements and the implications of contemporary nationalism. Ernest Renan,[13] a proponent of religious dominance over human development, asserted that the formation of European nations was a result of the assimilation and unity of their people through religion and language. He overlooked the fact that religion did not prevent the establishment of nation-states aligned with a single religious tradition or Christian denomination, nor did it stop them from engaging in violent conflicts. This did not deter major imperial states from exploiting religion, professing devotion to it, and claiming to defend its adherents as a means of infiltrating and occupying foreign lands. Tsarist Russia, for instance, proclaimed itself the protector of the Orthodox faith and supported the Bulgarian national struggle against the Ottoman Empire in order to secure influence in the nascent Bulgarian state. Simultaneously, it invoked the Bulgarians' belonging to the Slavic family of peoples to consolidate this process.

Imperial powers like Tsarist Russia and France divided the Christians of the Ottoman Arab provinces between them – Russia aligning with the Greek Orthodox and France with the Western Christian denominations – under the pretext of protectorates. This was, however, merely a preparatory phase for the eventual occupation of these provinces. Imperialism, however, abandoned religion when it conflicted with its interests: Britain, for example, refrained from supporting the Christian Greeks in their struggle for freedom and independence from the Ottoman Empire, and instead backed the Druze leadership during the 1860 massacres in Lebanon, showing indifference to the Christian victims.

When analysing the bourgeois period, Lenin emphasised the importance of distinguishing between two phases: the first being the rise of the bourgeoisie and the establishment of its nation-state (as previously mentioned), and the second, the transition period following the completion of the bourgeois states' formation. This latter phase is characterised by heightened class conflict and colonial expansion. During this second period, the bourgeoisie entered its imperial stage, achieving the peak of its economic and political influence and dominance in capitalist countries, thereby surpassing the nationalist ideologies it had once supported.

British Prime Minister Benjamin Disraeli, who witnessed the beginning of this era, expressed an ideology hostile to nationalism. He remarked, 'the con-

13 Ernest Renan (1823–92), French philosopher and historian, known for his influential writings on nationalism and the historical study of religion, especially *Qu'est-ce qu'une nation?* (1882). (A.K.)

cept of nationalism was created by a group of students who lack reason, and by fanatic teachers'.[14]

It is notable that the imperial powers, in their efforts to maintain control over their colonies, employed a 'divide and rule' strategy, often exacerbating national conflicts where possible and encouraging sectarian tensions when deemed advantageous. Colonial history offers abundant evidence of this approach. In India, for instance, British imperialism incited sectarian conflict between Hindus and Muslims, which ultimately led to the partition of the Indian subcontinent into two separate nations, India and Pakistan. In Palestine, colonial policies intensified the conflict between Arabs and Jews, resulting in the partition plan. Similarly, Cyprus continues to suffer from the legacy of British imperialism, which sowed discord between Turkish and Greek Cypriots.

However, religion was not always a reliable tool in the hands of imperial powers. In his analysis of the global impact of the 1905 Russian Revolution, Lenin noted that the democratic revolution extended throughout Asia. He observed:

> A significant development is the spread of the revolutionary democratic movement to the Dutch East Indies, to Java and the other Dutch colonies, with a population of some forty million. First, the democratic movement is developing among the masses of Java, where a nationalist movement has arisen under the banner of Islam ...[15]

It is well-known that after France began its colonisation of Algeria in 1830, it faced persistent and violent resistance, often led by nationalist leaders rallying under the banner of Islam. In response, the imperial authorities devoted significant effort to diminishing the influence of Islam, effectively launching a crusade against it. Throughout the national struggle, mosques and *kuttabs* (traditional Islamic schools for young children) became crucial centres for the Algerian nationalist movement. These institutions initially served as refuges for the movement and served as points of departure for its activities before the movement eventually evolved into a secular one.

The Muslim Scholars' Conference, held in Algeria at the peak of this period in 1936, played a key role in articulating revolutionary national demands, marking a significant moment in the country's revolutionary nationalist struggle.

---

14 Al-Husari 1963, p. 22.

15 Lenin 1913.

In this context, it is essential to note that the bourgeoisie, which rose to prominence in human history by leveraging nationalism and opposing religious forces, later turned to religion in its ideological battle against communism. After World War II, in an effort to counter the proletariat's struggle for socialism, the bourgeoisie utilised religion to form political parties in certain Western European countries for this purpose. Prominent examples include West Germany, where the bourgeoisie founded the Christian Democratic Party, which governed for more than two decades and continues to contend with the Social Democratic Party, which came to power a few years ago, and Italy, where the Christian Democratic Party remains at the centre of power.

CHAPTER 9

The Relationship between Religion and Nationalism in the Arab World

1 Two Parallel Currents

Since the establishment of the Islamic Arab Empire, intellectual and social movements – whether revolutionary or reactionary – have largely emerged from an Islamic religious rationale. Throughout Islamic history, religion has played a decisive role in both worldly and spiritual matters, shaping key relationships between humans and God, as well as between individuals within society.

The Ottoman Empire, which encompassed the territories that today constitute the Arab world, positioned itself as the legitimate heir of the Islamic Arab Empire. It adopted Islam, both in its administrative structures and religious practices, as a social and ideological framework. Nevertheless, the Ottoman Empire ultimately exhausted its capacity for development and, consequently, for survival. This outcome was shaped by two fundamental factors: first, the social struggle to dismantle the feudal economic system, and second, the national struggle, led by oppressed peoples, for liberty.

In the nineteenth century, these two factors – social and national – became particularly decisive throughout the Ottoman Empire. However, the balance between them varied across provinces. In non-Muslim provinces of the Balkans, the national struggle, often characterised by violent resistance, took precedence, while in the Arab provinces, the social struggle – marked by aspirations for reform – was more prominent.

This distribution was not coincidental. In the Balkans, where the population was predominantly Christian, the national struggle took on a distinctly Christian character. In contrast, the majority of the population in the Arab provinces was Muslim, and because Islamic principles were deeply intertwined with societal issues, people turned to these religious principles to advocate for social reforms. While the banner of independence was raised in Greece, Bulgaria, Montenegro, Bosnia, and other Balkan provinces, it was notably absent in the Arab Ottoman provinces. Even as Arab nationalism gained traction in these regions, Arab nationalist movements advocated for remaining under Ottoman rule, albeit with a call for decentralisation.

It is certain that news of the Great French Revolution (the classical bourgeois revolution that heralded nationalism and bourgeoisie) filtered into the

HTTPS://DOI.ORG/10.1163/9789004774261-014

Arab Ottoman provinces and left its mark on some Arab intellectuals. However, the interaction with the principles of this revolution was minimal. We can agree with the author of *al-Thawri al-ʿArabi al-ʿmuasir* (The Contemporary Arab Revolutionary) when he distinguished the first half of the nineteenth century by the emergence of two currents to confront the economic-political crisis that the Arab provinces were experiencing: 'The first considers religious reform as the foundation of social reform, while the second considers that social reform must necessarily reform religion'.[1]

It is important to note that many thinkers during this period based their rationale on Islam. Whether religious reform came first or second in their approach made little difference, as they believed religion surpassed all other considerations. ʿAbd al-Rahman al-Kawakibi, one of the most prominent Arab thinkers of the time, linked the decline of Muslims to distortions that had affected their religion. He thus called for religious reform, accompanied by political reform. Kawakibi argued that political tyranny stems from religious tyranny, and that religious tolerance fosters political tolerance.[2]

Even as nationalist sentiments grew among the people of the Arab provinces under Ottoman rule, driven in part by Turkish persecution and assertions of racial superiority, many intellectuals continued to view religion as a social framework for achieving reform. Muhammad ʿAbdu, a colleague of Jamal al-Din al-Afghani[3] and a prominent thinker of the period, articulated this perspective in al-ʿUrwa Al-Wuthqa (The Firmest Bond). He called for a return to the foundations of religion to correct societal vices, asserting that 'For the seed of religion is inherent in souls through heredity from long ages, and hearts are at peace with it ... Thus, one who undertakes to revive the nation needs only a single breath whose essence flows through all spirits ... And whoever seeks to reform a nation of such character as we have described by means other than this has embarked upon error and made the end a beginning'.[4]

1 Allush 1960, p. 23.

2 Al-Kawakibi 1902, p. 12.

3 Jamal al-Din al-Afghani (1838–97) – Influential Islamic modernist thinker and political activist. Born in Afghanistan (though some sources suggest Iran), he advocated for Islamic reform, pan-Islamic unity, and resistance to European colonialism. Traveled extensively throughout the Muslim world promoting educational reform and constitutional government. His ideas significantly influenced the Islamic reform movement and inspired later thinkers like Muhammad Abduh. Known for blending traditional Islamic thought with modern political and scientific concepts.

4 Rida 1921, p. 235.

For Muhammad ʿAbduh, the central issue was not one of form but of essence. He rejected the application of nationalism to Muslims. For this reason, he wrote in *al-ʿurwa al-wuthqa* that races were established on the basis of tribal solidarity (nationalism) because their members united to preserve their rights from the tyranny of a ruler from another race. However, the situation differs among Muslims, and he added: 'This is the secret behind Muslims' aversion, despite their different ethnicities, to considering racial distinctions and their rejection of any form of tribal solidarity except their Islamic bond. For one who is truly religious in the Islamic faith, once his belief becomes firmly rooted, becomes indifferent to his race and people and turns away from particular ties to universal relationships'.

In fact, the call for reform based on Islamic principles was progressive in both its internal and external dimensions. Internally, it opposed tyranny and ignorance, promoting democracy, ideological liberation, and social freedom. Externally, it declared war on British imperialism. Thus, the nationalist element became significant, even within the broader context of Islamic Daʿwa (mission). This was evident in Muhammad ʿAbduh's defence of Egypt's national rights against British dominance.

In Syria, where the Islamic religious current had initially prevailed, it began to recede in the face of the growth of nationalist sentiment on the one hand, and the dangers of sectarian conflict on the other. ʿAbd al-Rahman al-Kawakibi, whose nationalist leanings were evident in his call for an Arab – rather than Turkish – caliphate, was profoundly shaken by the sectarian massacres of the 1860s. As a result, he increasingly emphasised the national foundation binding Arabs together rather than the religious one. He wrote:

> O my people, and by you I mean those who speak in the tongue of ḍād [Arabic], even if they are not Muslims, I call upon you to forget the offenses and resentments, and the crimes of fathers and forefathers ... These nations of Australia and America have been guided by science to diverse paths and established sound principles of national union rather than religious union, of ethnic (national) concord rather than sectarian concord, of political association rather than administrative.

And after warning against the foreign and non-Arab agitators who incite discord, he added:

> Let us, O people, manage our affairs in eloquent Arabic, understand one another in fraternity, console one another in adversity, and be equal in prosperity. Let us govern our worldly life, and leave religions to judge in the hereafter alone. Let us

> come together upon a common word, and that word is: long live the nation, long live the homeland, let us live as free men.[5]

With the emergence of the Arab nationalist movement in the Ottoman Arab provinces at the beginning of the twentieth century, the Islamic current began to recede in favour of the growing nationalist current. Pioneers and various social forces active in political life – including merchants, physicians, lawyers, and the enlightened sons of feudalists – came to believe that the social reform sought by the nascent Arab bourgeoisie in Syria was intrinsically linked to 'national reform'. This meant gaining acknowledgment of Arab national rights from the Ottoman Empire, including the right to self-governance, the use of the Arabic language, and the implementation of essential administrative reforms. The nationalist movement surpassed the Islamic religious current, culminating in the first Arab congress held by Arab nationalists in Paris in 1913.

In his speech at the congress, ʿAbdul Hamid al-Zahrawi[6] addressed this issue, stating that religious unity had failed to achieve political unity. It had also failed to resolve even simple disputes, such as the border conflict between the Ottoman and Persian governments. He argued that Arab nationalists did not advocate for political unity solely for religious reasons but rather out of a desire to form a national Ottoman group rooted in the Arab community, one that could develop and thrive without obstruction.[7] This sentiment was echoed by other speakers at the congress, notably ʿAbd al-Ghani al-ʿAraysi,[8] who cited scholars from various nations and concluded that 'all scholars agree that Arabs have the right to be a complete social entity, with a shared language, history, and culture, to form a cohesive political community, and to achieve independence as a nation'.[9]

During World War I, when Arab nationalism confronted Ottoman authority and many nationalist leaders were executed, ʿAbd al-Ghani al-ʿAraysi – one of those executed – called for unity among Arabs. He wrote, 'We must no longer be

5 Al-Kawakibi 1902, p. 110.

6 Abdul Hamid al-Zahrawi (1855–1916) was a Syrian Arab nationalist, writer, and political activist who advocated for Arab rights within the Ottoman Empire, served as a member of the Ottoman Parliament, and was executed by Ottoman authorities in 1916 during the crackdown on Arab nationalist leaders. (A.K.)

7 Said 1930, p. 513.

8 ʿAbd al-Ghanī al-ʿAraysī (1891–1916) was a Lebanese journalist and Arab nationalist, and one of the intellectuals executed by Jamal Pasha on 6 May 1916, in what became known as Martyrs' Day.

9 Ibid., 515.

divided into Christian, Muslim, Jewish, Druze, or Hamawi. The ideological path of Beirut is the same for Lebanon, the Levant, Aleppo, Palestine, Iraq, Hijaz, and Yemen'.[10]

This vision of nationalism transcended territorial and sectarian boundaries, even in the early days of the Arab nationalist movements. Its significance lies in its challenge to the religious unity championed by the Ottoman authorities. It was well-known that Sultan Abdulhamid II, at the turn of the twentieth century, had raised the banner of Islamic unity, hoping to use it as a barrier against the growing Arab nationalist movement. This movement had risen due to economic-social development in the Arab provinces and was strengthened after the 1908 revolution, which brought the Turkish bourgeois current to power in the Ottoman Empire and inaugurated an era of Turkish chauvinist nationalist practices against all ethnic groups, including the Arab nation, which was not helped by the fact that its overwhelming majority belonged to Islam.

2 The Blend of Religion and Nationalism

The intense confrontation between Arabs and Turks led to the triumph of the nationalist current over the Islamic one in the Ottoman Arab provinces. However, other Arab provinces did not experience such direct conflicts with the Ottomans but instead engaged in fierce battles with imperial powers. In particular, the French imperialists, who conquered Algeria in 1830 and Tunisia in 1881, viewed Islam as their greatest enemy in their efforts to suppress the popular resistance to occupation in both countries. In this context, adherence to Islam – especially in response to the superficial and aggressive form of Christianity promoted by the imperialists – became an integral part of nationalism.

This phenomenon dates back to the early stages of Arab nationalism, when nationalism was still in its primal or even tribal form, as seen in Algeria, for example. During this period, 'Islam was at the heart of many Arabs, substituting for nationalism, and the solidarity of Islamic fraternity replaced the sense of nationalist solidarity'.[11]

Considering this, it becomes clear why religion remained a key component of nationalist movements in the Arab Maghreb – Algeria, Morocco, Tunisia, and

10 *Thawrat al-ʿArab, Muqaddimatuha – Asbabuha – Nataʾijiha* [The Arab Revolt: Its Preliminaries – Its Causes – Its Results] (Cairo: Al-Muqattam Print House, n.d.), p. 244.

11 Hussein Muhammad Tawfiq, *Hadha al-ʿAlam al-ʿArabi* [This Arab World] (Beirut: Dar al-ʿIlm lil-Malayin, 1953), p. 47.

Libya – without negatively affecting the struggle led by these movements. In Algeria, for example, the Association of Algerian Muslim Ulama, established in 1928, played a major role in encouraging nationalist forces in the 1930s to adopt an ideology that fused nationalism with religion. The Association declared: 'The Algerian Nation exists as a complete entity, like all other nations on earth. It continues to exist, with its rich history, religious and linguistic identity, and its own culture, including both positive and negative customs ….'[12]

This religious component persisted and became even more pronounced during nationalist struggles. When the 'Committee for the Liberation of the Maghreb' was formed in Cairo in 1947, its charter affirmed that the Arab Maghreb had been founded through Islam, survived through Islam, and would continue on the path of Islam. It also declared that the Maghreb was an integral part of the Arab world, and that its cooperation with the Arab League – like all Arab countries – was both natural and necessary. The charter emphasised that the independence of the Maghreb should apply equally to the three regions: Tunisia, Algeria, and Morocco.[13] The document also underscored the unity of these regions through 'language, religion, ethnicity, history, geography, colonialism, and the shared aspiration for liberation'.[14]

It is important to highlight that the religious component did not arise solely in response to imperialist attacks, particularly those by Christian missionaries attempting to convert Muslims. Rather, it was also an indicator of social development in the region. As the nationalist revival continued, and the Arab element of nationalism became more pronounced due to shifts in social forces, the prominence of this religious component gradually diminished, as seen in the activities of the National Liberation Front. The growing influence of the proletariat and popular classes within the nationalist movement further weakened the religious element, and intensified consciousness purified from metaphysical elements, whether racial or religious.

The persistence of the religious element in national affairs across the Arab world, whether viewed positively or negatively, reflects the enduring influence of feudal ideology, which preceded the rise of nationalism. When nationalism emerged and confronted feudalism, it did not fully replace it. Instead, it blended with Islamic religious ideology, often without distinguishing between the two. The use of religion – or selective interpretations of it – to resist revolutionary currents is neither new nor unexpected.

12 Quoted in Al-Qasi 1947, p. 17.
13 Al-Qasi 1947, p. 409.
14 Al-Qasi 1947, p. 407.

Indeed, reactionary forces used the concept of Islamic unity to oppose the Great Socialist Revolution, which triumphed in Tsarist Russia and sparked a wave of political and social revolutions worldwide. However, the concept of Islamic unity, which had been overshadowed by Arab nationalism during the twentieth century, re-emerged not as Jamal al-Din al-Afghani had envisioned – a tool to unite Arab nations against European imperialism – but as a disguised mechanism to block revolutionary paths, particularly to curb the influence of the Great Socialist Revolution.

One of the prominent proponents of Islamic unity during this period was Muhammad Rashid Rida, author of *al-Khilafa aw al-Imama al-ʿUzma* (The Caliphate or the Great Imamate), which called for the establishment of an Islamic government to 'thwart the Bolshevik threat'. After describing the precarious state of the world, Reda wrote: 'People urgently need continuous civil and religious reform to end the marginalisation and exploitation of the poor by the rich, to counter the Bolshevik threat to the wealthy, and to eliminate ethnic discrimination in order to achieve fraternity among all peoples. This can only be accomplished through an Islamic government'.[15]

However, such calls for Islamic unity could not withstand the rise of nationalist movements in the Arab world. Although the Islamic component persisted within these movements, the ideology of Arab nationalism increasingly aligned with contemporary nationalist ideologies. Over time, it began to shed elements of occultism, both religious and non-religious.

3 The Muslim Brotherhood in Confrontation with Arab Nationalism

While Muhammad Rashid Rida's call for Islamic unity faded away, the question of Islam's role in opposition to nationalism grew in reactionary circles in Egypt. This idea gained further traction with the rise of the Muslim Brotherhood. As noted by Muhammad Shawqi in his book *Al-Ikhwan al-Muslimun wal-Mujtamaʿ al-Misri* (*The Muslim Brotherhood and Egyptian Society*), the Brotherhood emerged from a small group founded by Sheikh Hassan al-Banna in March 1928. Despite the efforts and publications of al-Banna, the Muslim Brotherhood initially remained a marginal force, particularly in rural areas, and had little impact on Egyptian society.[16]

15 Rida 1922, p. 7.
16 Shawqi 1954.

However, the period of World War II (1939–1945) marked a turning point, during which this once-marginal organisation grew into a nationwide movement. The Muslim Brotherhood began to actively engage in the Egyptian political arena, both internally and externally. It soon became evident that the ruling authorities, who had facilitated the Brotherhood's rise, intended to use the organisation as a tool to curb Egypt's revolutionary momentum. This followed the intensification of social and national conflict, alongside increased class and political polarisation, particularly after the defeat of the Nazis in World War II and the rise of revolutionary movements worldwide, especially in colonies and semi-colonies. For this reason, it was no coincidence that the Muslim Brotherhood organisation adopted slogans of equality and spoke about the rights of workers and peasants with rhetorical demagoguery, as this was their way of standing against the Communists.

As the struggle against imperialism and the push for national liberation escalated, the Muslim Brotherhood sought to distort the nationalist vision by promoting the concept of 'Islamic nationalism'. Hassan al-Banna, the Brotherhood's leader, argued that the group did not confine its national identity to territorial or geographic boundaries. He wrote:

> The Muslim Brotherhood does not limit national borders to territorial and geographical boundaries, for every place where a Muslim resides is sacred, and all Muslims, regardless of their geographical location, are our people and brothers, whom we care for and sympathize with. As for the pretentious patriots (and here he means nationalism – E.T.), they are not like us; they only care for narrow lands.[17]

It is important to distinguish between the members of the Muslim Brotherhood and its leadership. Many members, regardless of their organisational affiliation, fought alongside nationalist groups on various battlefronts – in Egypt, Syria, and elsewhere – driven by nationalist convictions. However, the leadership collaborated with local reactionary forces and was often aligned with imperialist powers. It is well-known that the assassinations of Egyptian Prime Minister Fahmi al-Nuqrashi[18] and Muslim Brotherhood leader Hassan al-Banna occurred within the broader context of the Anglo-American struggle.

---

17 Hassan al-Banna, *Al-Rasa'il Al-Thalath – Daʿwatuna* [The Three Treatises – Our Call], quoted in Shawqi 1954, p. 59.

18 Fahmi al-Nuqrashi (1888–1948) was an Egyptian nationalist and Prime Minister, affiliated with the Wafd and later the Saadist Institutional Party. He served two terms (1945–6, 1946–8) and was assassinated by a member of the Muslim Brotherhood in December 1948. (A.K.)

Among the indicators of rising nationalist sentiments during this period was the Muslim Brotherhood's declaration regarding their national affiliation. In the booklet *Daʿwatuna fi Tawr Jadid* (*Our mission in its new phase*), Hassan al-Banna emphasised:

> We are proud of our loyalty to this homeland; we work for it, we love it, and we struggle for its welfare, and we will continue to do so as long as we exist. We believe that this is the first step in the broader revival we aspire to, and that Egypt is an integral part of the Arab world. By serving Egypt's interests, we also serve the interests of Arabism, the Orient, and Islam (Ibid., p. 59).

It is evident that the advocates of Islamic or Islamic-national unity in the Arab world were influenced by Arab nationalism, often echoing the traditional slogan: the dignity of the Arabs is inseparable from the dignity of Islam, and vice versa. This perspective is why Hassan al-Banna wrote in *Daʿwatuna fi Tawr Jadid*: 'Islam cannot progress unless Arab unity and progress are achieved, and every inch of Arab land is, for us, the heart and core of our homeland'. He further emphasised that 'geographical boundaries and political divisions cannot tear apart the Islamic-Arab unity'.[19]

4 The Triumph of Nationalism and its Abandonment by Reactionism which Returned to Religion

The rise of the Muslim Brotherhood reached its peak in Egypt – where its influence was most notable – before the Revolution of July 23, 1952. However, following the revolution, the movement experienced a steady decline, and the organisation, which aspired to become a popular movement, fragmented into various factions with differing approaches but a shared fate. The 1950s saw the retreat of the idea of Islamic unity or Islamic nationalism, as the Arab nationalist movement emerged as a revolutionary giant, both regionally and globally. This movement had a profound impact on nationalist movements in Africa and contributed significantly to the global revolutionary process. Arab nationalism became the driving force behind several key events: the Algerian Revolution, the nationalisation of the Suez Canal, a wave of popular identification across the Arab world, the formation of the United Arab Republic between Syria and Egypt, the July 14th 1958 revolution in Iraq, and the broader Arab resurgence.

19 Shawqi 1954, pp. 59–60.

This momentum led to the establishment of the Arab League in 1945, at the end of World War II, as an embodiment of the Arab nations' aspirations for unity. However, the League failed to fully achieve its mission, particularly in leading the struggle for national liberation and independence. Reflecting the political dynamics of the Arab governments it represented, the League became a battleground between the ruling elites and the two major imperial powers – Britain and the United States – competing for dominance over the Arab countries. The League's failures were further exacerbated by its inability to effectively address the Palestinian cause, which became a central issue in Arab politics.

Though weakened, the League still represented the idea of Arab nationalism, contributing to the establishment of the United Arab Republic between Egypt and Syria, founded on the principle of Arab unity with the goal of achieving a comprehensive union. While a detailed analysis of the stages leading to this union is beyond the scope of this discussion, it is clear that the proposal of Arab unity marked a decisive new phase in the relationship between nationalism and religion. This shift favoured Arab nationalism unequivocally, excluding religion from the political sphere, and reflected the prevailing sentiment across the Arab world, where nationalist ideals were embraced by members of various religions within the Arab nations, or the broader Great Arab Nation.

The triumph of Arab nationalism was closely tied to its association with anti-imperialism and its commitment to profound social reform. Given this, it is not surprising that reactionary forces within the Arab world united in opposition to Arab nationalism, calling for a return to religious faith – whether Muslim or Christian. This reactionary stance was exemplified by the newspaper *Al-Hayat*, established in Beirut and associated with imperialist reactionary circles. In 1966, the paper argued that Arab nationalism could not succeed, claiming it was influenced by Marxism and was merely the doctrine of Marxist Arabs. It suggested that nationalism had already achieved its goals and had nothing more to offer, advocating instead for a return to religious faith as an effective, yet underutilised, weapon in the fight against Marxism.

However, the relationship between religion and nationalism does not end here. The victory of nationalism did not mean that social forces – particularly reactionary ones – would cease using religion to pursue their objectives. Furthermore, some forces that appeared progressive and even contributed to anti-imperialist struggles also turned to religion, either because they misunderstood the true nature of nationalism or out of genuine belief in the power of religion (specifically Islam) to shape social and political life.

One notable example is the constitution of the Egyptian-Syrian-Libyan union, declared in Damascus in August 1971. The constitution stated that Islam would serve as the source of legislation, although many prominent Arab thinkers (mostly Muslims) argued that religious foundations were inadequate for addressing the complexities of modern life. The inclusion of religion in the legislative process stemmed from the belief held by some Arab nationalists that one of the core components of Arab nationalism was 'unified legislation' across the Arab world, derived from Islamic law.[20]

Thus, while the balance of political activism in the Arab world continues to favour Arab nationalism, religion remains an element reintroduced by reactionary forces, particularly those aligned with imperialism. In the best-case scenarios, religion is utilised to further conservative agendas, but it is often deployed by forces that collaborate with imperialist interests.

20 Darawzah, p. 85.

CHAPTER 10

Sectarianism under Ottoman Rule

The Quran, in many Surahs, references the presence of various religious groups and sects in the Arabian Peninsula, and it takes a clear stance on these groups across two interconnected levels: the religious and the civil.

At the religious level, the Quranic verses converse with the People of the Book and call them to convert to Islam – the religion of truth – interceding with them and providing them with protection. For example:

> And do not argue with the People of the Scripture except in a way that is best, except for those who commit injustice among them, and say, We believe in that which has been revealed to us and revealed to you. And our God and your God is one; and we are Muslims [in submission] to Him. (Quran 29:46).

A verse in al-Baqara chapter states:

> Indeed, those who believed and those who were Jews or Christians or Sabeans [before Prophet Muhammad] – those [among them] who believed in Allah and the Last Day and did righteousness – will have their reward with their Lord, and no fear will there be concerning them, nor will they grieve. (Quran 2:62)

Yet, a verse in Al-Ma'idah chapter differentiates between Jews and Christians:

> You will surely find the most intense of the people in animosity toward the believers [to be] the Jews and those who associate others with Allah; and you will find the nearest of them in affection to the believers those who say, 'We are Christians'. That is because among them are priests and monks and because they are not arrogant. (Quran 5:82).

At the civil level, the Quran presents a decisive position towards the *People of the Book*, specifically in the chapter *At-Taubah*:

> Fight those who do not believe in Allah or in the Last Day and who do not consider unlawful what Allah and His Messenger have made unlawful and who do not adopt the religion of truth from those who were given the Scripture – [fight] until they give the jizyah willingly while they are humbled (Quran 9:29).

 | HTTPS://DOI.ORG/10.1163/9789004774261-015

No significant difference is found between the religious and civil levels, especially since the examples illustrating the relationship between religious matters and civil affairs, or between a person's connection to God and their relationship to Islam in daily life, were spontaneous and natural. However, the events that unfolded in the Islamic Arab Empire show that the ruling elites, along with intellectuals, often chose the more flexible and tolerant Quranic verses when dealing with the *People of the Book*, and even with Zoroastrians. They demonstrated considerable tolerance in their approach, dialogue, and human interaction. Nevertheless, the civil attitude toward non-Muslims was evident in the imposition of the *jizyah* – a tax applied by the new system, which signified the special relationship between Muslims and non-Muslims. This component of the civil system was part of a broader framework that outlined the rights and obligations of non-Muslims.

Historian Philip Hitti attributes the decrees that governed the relationship between Muslims and non-Muslims to the Umayyad Caliph, ʿUmar ibn ʿAbd al-ʿAziz (r. 717–720 CE). Among the most notable of these decrees were those that prohibited Christians from holding official positions, disallowed their testimony in court, banned the construction of churches and monasteries, and imposed distinct clothing and behavioural regulations. As a result, Christians – and apparently Jews as well – were forbidden from resembling Muslims. For instance, they were not allowed to wear turbans or belts, nor were they permitted to ride on saddles, but instead had to use pack saddles.[1]

Despite these regulations, divisions between Muslims and non-Muslims were not always strictly enforced. In fact, sectarian tensions within the Muslim community were often more intense and violent than those between Muslims and Christians or Jews. The Shiʿa, for example, endured severe persecution at various points in Islamic-Arab history, while historical accounts tend to focus less on the treatment of Jews and Christians by the ruling authorities. Many prominent Jewish and Christian scholars held significant positions, benefiting from Islamic tolerance, which continued until the Ottoman Turks assumed the Caliphate. After that, religious fanaticism became more prevalent, aligned with the socio-political structure shaped by Eastern feudalism, which emerged due to specific historical developments.

However, this fanaticism did not renew or change the relationships between the various factions; instead, it deepened the separation and isolation, rather than mitigating it. This development aligned with the feudal system, which was based on division and segregation. Thus, the debate surrounding sectar-

1 Hitti 1952, p. 302.

ianism during that period, which persisted for a long time, centred on two main axes: discriminatory treatment and social isolation in human relationships.

Evidently, this situation was far from ideal. The restrictions imposed on non-Muslims relegated them to second-class citizenship, preventing them from fully participating in social life and limiting their freedoms. Yet, this did not lead to outright sectarian conflict. Furthermore, reactionary forces at the time did not exploit religious fanaticism to the extent that it would provoke religious conflicts and distract people from pressing issues. In this context, it is no coincidence that Salah al-Din (Saladin), during his battles against the Crusaders, found allies and supporters among Arab Christians. These Christians rejected the Crusaders' claims of 'rescuing the holy places from heretics' and resented the so-called 'religious fraternity' promoted by the Crusaders, which masked national arrogance and ethnic disdain toward the local population.

When the Ottoman Empire took control of Arab lands (2) in the fifteenth and sixteenth centuries, it encountered challenges regarding non-Muslim populations in regions such as the Fertile Crescent (Iraq and Greater Syria, which includes Syria, Lebanon, Palestine, and Transjordan) and Egypt. In contrast, the remaining 'Ottoman' Arab provinces were characterised by significant divisions within Islam itself.

Following a system that had existed in both the Byzantine Empire and the Islamic Arab Empire, the Ottomans established the 'Millet' system. This system granted religious communities a considerable degree of autonomy, particularly concerning religious matters and personal status (such as marriage, divorce, and inheritance). Historians note that this system allowed conservative and reactionary religious leaders (3) to exert tight control over their followers, strengthening the authority of the *'Ulama* (Muslim scholars) within the Ottoman Empire. These scholars played a significant role in suppressing reforms during the nineteenth century, hindering the modernisation process. Additionally, they were instrumental in the reactionary movements that emerged after the Democratic Bourgeois Revolution in Turkey in 1908, briefly achieving their reactionary goals.

Local and global events contributed to the decline of the feudal system in the Ottoman Empire, with the most significant being the emergence of the Arab-Egyptian regime in Syria, following the victory of Ibrahim Pasha's campaign (4) (1831–40).

Most historians agree that this Arab-Egyptian regime achieved a degree of equality among all religions, dealing a heavy blow to the feudalists and local traditional leaders. It also initiated agricultural and industrial development processes that could have steered society toward a capitalist phase. However, the colonial Ottoman intervention was decisive in eliminating this regime. Nonetheless, this event raised awareness among Ottoman officials regarding the urgent need for reform and to address the Empire's growing backwardness, especially considering the upheavals in Europe, where two revolutions – the governance-related bourgeois revolution and the industrial revolution – had dramatically transformed society and production methods.

The spread of democratic bourgeois ideas, particularly after the French Revolution (1789), also brought about significant changes. At the same time, colonial powers sought to seize Ottoman provinces, using various levels of intervention, including sectarian ones. Thus, by the middle of the nineteenth century, Tsarist Russia declared itself the protector of the Orthodox community regardless of where they were located or their national affiliation. It was the protector of the Orthodox Bulgarians in Bulgaria and the Orthodox Arabs in Syria. During the same period, France openly proclaimed its right to protect the Catholic community in the 'Ottoman' Arab East, and it was not troubled by the fact that it had separated religion from the state since its great revolution and had become completely secular.

As Protestants were largely absent from the Arab world, Protestant Britain found itself without a religious group to align with. Thus, it decided to support the Druze community. In his book *The Near East*, Yale William wrote, 'In Syria where British economic interests were less important than those of the French, and in Lebanon where the powerful Maronites (Roman Catholics) were French proteges, the British, as a means of counterbalancing French influence there, gave their support to the Druzes'.[2]

As Satiʿ al-Husri remarked, it was impossible for the situation to remain static in the first half of the nineteenth century, a period characterised by national and popular revolutions. This dynamic opened the door to civil revolutions on one hand and European interventions on the other.[3] Ottoman reforms took the form of two significant decrees. The first was issued in 1839, known as the 'Edict of Gülhane' or 'The Hatt-ı Hümayun', and the second was 'Imperial Reform Edict', issued in 1856 under Sultan Abdülmecid I (1839–1861). The core of these decrees focused on establishing democratic bourgeois rights, ensuring human freedom and equality under the law. The first decree safeguarded 'security of life, dignity, and property', prohibited arbitrary confiscation of property, and banned punishment without trial. The second decree enshrined 'equal

---

2 Yale 1958, p. 60. (A.K.)
3 Al-Husari 1965, p. 89.

treatment for all subjects of the state (i.e., its citizens), regardless of their religions or sects', without infringing upon the rights and privileges of non-Muslim leaders.[4]

Despite these reforms, they did not eliminate religious divisions or significantly bring adherents of different religions closer together. In fact, sectarianism increased, as reactionary forces within each religion feared losing control over their followers and saw the potential collapse of their dominance if members of different religions cooperated for their collective benefit. Sectarian tensions were further exacerbated by the influx of Christian missionaries – who served as the cultural-religious vanguard of colonial powers – into the region. They established schools and promoted the use of the Arabic language at a time when state (imperial) schools attended primarily by Muslims were limited to instruction in Turkish.

The teaching of Arabic literature and language in missionary schools helped spread Arab culture more effectively among Christian Arabs than among Muslim Arabs. Consequently, it was no surprise that Arab nationalism spread more widely and earlier among Christian Arabs in the Fertile Crescent. Meanwhile, the Ottoman Empire sought to prevent Arab nationalism from taking hold among Muslims, promoting the idea that it was a continuation of the Islamic Caliphate. The Empire succeeded, for a time, in convincing Muslims that they were part of the ruling power, though this notion was later refuted. To undermine unity among Arabs, the Ottoman Empire stoked national and religious tensions, as Philip Hitti points out in his book *History of the Arabs*, particularly in Lebanon between the Druze and Maronites.[5]

The first significant sectarian conflict erupted after the Egyptian forces withdrew from Syria in 1840. At that time, the Ottoman Empire sought to dismantle the Emirate of Mount Lebanon, led by Emir Bashir Shihab II,[6] who had supported Ibrahim Pasha's campaign, and return the region to centralised Ottoman control. The conflict, however, took place within the broader context of intense social class struggles. After the Egyptian withdrawal, prominent Druze feudalists returned to Lebanon to find that Maronite peasants had taken over their lands. Armed conflict ensued, with Druze reactionaries using weapons

4 Al-Husari 1965, pp. 87–8.

5 Hitti 1952, p. 864.

6 Bashir Shihab II (1767–1850) was the last feudal ruler of Mount Lebanon, governing from 1788 to 1840. Initially a Sunni Muslim who later converted to Maronite Christianity, he allied with Muhammad Ali Pasha of Egypt during the latter's occupation of Syria (1831–1840). After the Egyptian withdrawal and Ottoman restoration, he was exiled to Malta and later to Istanbul, marking the end of the Shihab dynasty's rule in Lebanon. (A.K.)

supplied by Britain.[7] The violence escalated, resulting in heavy casualties, particularly among Christians.

In 1845, reactionary forces once again incited sectarian conflict, exploiting the class struggle between Druze feudalists and Maronite peasants. In this round, both sides committed massacres against each other, with Maronite exterminating Druze peasants and vice versa. These events served the interests of the feudal system and the imperial powers, who intervened under the guise of restoring security to impose their own solutions and further entrench their presence.

However, the cruellest and most dangerous conflict occurred in 1860, known as the Massacres of 1860. The Soviet orientalist V. Lutski, in his book *Modern History of Arab Countries*, argues that the primary cause of the counter-revolutionary revolt against feudalism, which led to the sectarian massacres, was 'The Regulations of the Imperial Edict' of 1856. He explains that Lebanese peasants viewed the edict as a document calling for civil equality and as a sign of their liberation from feudal obligations. Indeed, representatives from the villages of Kesrawan met and presented their demands to the governor, focusing on the removal of all feudal restrictions. When the governor refused, the peasants, led by Tanyus Shahin,[8] launched an armed revolt in December 1859 and succeeded in expelling the Maronite feudal lords from Kesrawan. The revolutionary movement against feudalism spread to other regions of Lebanon, causing alarm among Druze feudalists over the threat to their class-based interests. In response, they armed factions of Druze volunteers, which ultimately led to the eruption of the massacre. The great social, or 'popular', revolt was thus drowned in a sectarian bloodbath.

The sectarian massacres of 1860 claimed the lives of more than 20,000 people and destroyed hundreds of villages on both sides. France, acting as the 'protector of the Maronites', successfully intervened in Ottoman affairs and gained international 'legitimacy' by deploying its forces along the Lebanese coast.[9]

---

7 Lutsky 1971, p. 153.

8 Tanyus Shahin (1815–95) was a Maronite blacksmith from the village of Rayfoun in the Keserwan district of Mount Lebanon who led the 1859 peasant uprising against feudal lords. His rebellion successfully expelled Maronite feudal families from Keserwan and established a form of peasant self-government. Though initially successful, the uprising was eventually suppressed by Ottoman and French intervention, and Shahin was exiled. He is remembered as a symbol of social revolution and peasant resistance against feudalism in Lebanese history. (A.K.)

9 Lutsky 1971, 161–4.

There is no doubt that the Ottoman Empire played an active role in escalating the sectarian conflict to strengthen its position, particularly in Mount Lebanon, which had long enjoyed autonomy. However, imperialist powers benefited even more, as they imposed a special status on Lebanon, thereby opening the door for greater foreign influence.

It is also worth noting that the French forces deployed along the Lebanese coast turned their anger toward the Maronite peasants who had rebelled against the feudal lords. The French returned the land to the feudalists and appointed their leader, Youssef Karam, as *qa'immaqam* (commissioner) of Kesrawan.

The Arab nationalist movement faced the challenge of overcoming religious divisions and finding a basis for unity between adherents of different faiths. This was achieved when Muslim and Christian pioneers cast aside old legacies of prejudice, religious fanaticism, and ideological narrowness. They recognised that Ottoman tyranny under Sultan Abdul Hamid II, alongside imperialist powers and sectarian reactionary forces, was hindering the Arab people's progress toward sociopolitical liberation.

This awareness was powerfully demonstrated at the first Arab Congress in Paris in 1913, where the rallying cry was: 'We are Arabs, and there is no distinction between Muslims and non-Muslims; we are Arabs before being Muslims or Christians'. Yet, sectarianism continues to serve as a reactionary tool, still exploited by imperialist powers to divide the Arab world.

CHAPTER 11

Sectarianism – A Tool for Imperialism and Reactionism

The British and French imperialists achieved their objectives after World War I (1914–1918) when they seized control of the Arab provinces of the Ottoman Empire. These provinces were divided between them through covert conflicts[1] and the manipulative manoeuvres that characterise imperialist powers. Iraq, Palestine, and Transjordan fell under British control, while Syria and Lebanon were allocated to France.[2]

While Britain and France had used sectarianism during Ottoman rule to infiltrate the Ottoman Arab provinces, after their occupation of these territories, sectarianism became a tool to divide the nation and consolidate their presence according to the ancient Roman principle: 'divide and rule'. In this endeavour, the two imperial powers found a reliable ally in Arab reactionism, composed of feudal parties and religious fanatics.

1 Sectarianism in Palestine

Although the British relied heavily on provoking racial conflict between Arabs and Jews in Palestine to consolidate control, they did not abandon sectarianism. They made every effort to divide the Arab Palestinian people into factions. More dangerously, during the British Mandate, the authorities did not recognise the Arabs as a national entity and sought to distribute local governance seats based on sectarian affiliation. When they proposed establishing a legislative council, representation was to be divided between Muslims, Jews, and Christians.

In the early period of the British Mandate, nationalist activism, influenced by British imperialism and reactionary parties, manifested as cooperation

1 Among these was Britain's exploitation of Faisal al-Hashemi, who was proclaimed king of Syria, in order to extract the oil-rich Mosul from French control and annex it to Iraq under British dominance.

2 We employ these geopolitical terminologies as imposed by the two imperialist powers following their domination of the region. Prior to this, the area extending from Iraq in the north to Sinai in the south constituted a single economic unit, which the Ottoman Sultanate had divided into provinces for administrative purposes.

 | HTTPS://DOI.ORG/10.1163/9789004774261-016

between Muslim and Christian institutions. However, the growing enthusiasm for national struggle sidelined this organisational structure, giving way to a nationalist framework, particularly in the 1920s, based on Arab nationalism. Its leadership emerged from national congresses held consecutively by nationalist activists. Although sectarian organisations did not disappear, they focused on their religious and charitable affairs, leaving the nationalist agenda to the executive committee.[3]

In the 1930s, with the establishment of nationalist parties, sectarianism largely faded, though some party leaders still considered sectarian aspects when forming their supreme institutions. Another factor contributing to the decline of sectarianism in Palestine was the widespread fear among the Arab public of the growing Imperialist-Zionist threat, which intensified during the 1930s following the influx of Jewish immigrants after the Nazi influence rose in Germany, which pursued brutal, racist, and antisemitic policies against Jewish residents.

What sustained a degree of sectarianism, though weak, in the Arab nationalist movement in Palestine was the nature of its religious leadership, particularly under Hajj Amin al-Husseini.[4] This leadership struggled to respond to the major events of the time and failed to propose a democratic solution to the Palestinian issue, as progressive forces called for independence and the establishment of an independent, democratic government where Arabs and Jews would be equal citizens.

2 France Resorts to Sectarianism in a Ridiculous Way

The way France and Britain wielded the reactionary weapon of sectarianism differed, depending on the conditions that prevailed in the regions dominated by these two imperialist powers. When France seized its share of the former Ottoman provinces, it immediately began dividing the region along sectarian lines, both publicly and privately.

---

3 The Executive Committee of the Palestinian Arab leadership during the British Mandate was a central representative body composed of prominent religious leaders, influential landowning families, and nationalist intellectuals from major cities and rural areas. It coordinated political and diplomatic activities, represented Palestinian interests before the British authorities, and sought to address issues related to land, immigration, and civil rights. (A.K.)

4 Haj Amin al-Husseini (1897–1974) was a Palestinian Arab nationalist and religious leader who served as Grand Mufti of Jerusalem from 1921 to 1948. He played a central role in Palestinian resistance to British Mandate policies and Zionist settlement, leading the 1936–39 Arab Revolt.

The public sectarian division aimed to fragment the Arab people into Muslims and Christians. Privately, France further fragmented these groups into various sects. The first step was the separation of 'Greater Lebanon' from Syria, establishing an independent entity composed of Mount Lebanon and the surrounding areas of Sidon, Tyre, Marjayoun, Tripoli, Akkar, Baalbek, Hasbaya, Rashaya, and Beqaa.

One of the primary motives behind this French imperialist move was the supposed interest in protecting Christian denominations, particularly the Maronites (the majority), while at the same time ensuring a significant Muslim population within this new entity. These motives became evident when the Lebanese constitution[5] distributed major political positions based on religious sects. For example, the president of the republic was required to be Maronite, the prime minister a Sunni Muslim, the speaker of the parliament a Shiite Muslim (from Jabal Amil), and parliamentary seats were allocated to members of all religious sects according to specific quotas.

What is important here is that France declared the independence of the Lebanese state on the 1st of September 1920,[6] and then advanced into Interior Syria,[7] which it occupied after suppressing the nationalist movement's attempt to secure independence that same year. While the coastal region of Syria was used to create 'Greater Lebanon', uniting the traditional 'Maronite' Mount Lebanon with various 'Muslim' regions that had never been part of Mount Lebanon, France divided inland Syria into smaller states based on Islamic sects. This was part of an effort to fragment the Arab people and weaken the nationalist movement by shifting their focus from broader concerns to narrower, sectarian-driven regional issues.

On the 8th of September 1920, the French High Commissioner declared the 'State of Aleppo' and appointed Kamel al-Qudsi, a collaborator with French imperialism, as its governor. On the 23rd of September 1920, the commissioner established the 'Alawite State' in the Latakia governorate and surrounding areas. Following the creation of the Alawite state, the state of Sunni Muslims was established in Damascus – declared on December 3, 1920, by one of the

5 Here Tuma conflates the Lebanese Constitution with the "National Pact" (al-Mithaq al-Watani), an unwritten agreement between representatives of the bourgeoisie from different Lebanese sects that divided the three fundamental positions according to sectarian distribution: a Maronite president, a Sunni prime minister, and a Shi'a speaker of parliament. (A.K.)

6 Tuma is referring to the declaration of the establishment of Greater Lebanon, not its independence, of course, which would only be achieved in 1943. (A.K.)

7 Following the partition, the Arab press came to refer to Lebanon as Coastal Syria, Palestine as Southern Syria, and what remained of Natural Syria as Interior Syria.

loyalists to French imperialism, Haqqi al-Azm. On the 20th of December 1920, in cooperation with certain Druze leaders, France declared the establishment of the 'Jabal Druze State' in the mountainous region bearing that name.

To further their strategy of division, the French High Commissioner also separated in 1924, the Sanjak of Alexandretta from the 'State of Aleppo', granting it systemic and administrative autonomy. However, the nationalist movement did not yield in the face of this dual division – first, the division of Arab regions between the two imperial powers, and second, the internal divisions imposed by France in the provinces under its control – and continued its struggle for national unity and independence.

When Britain and France agreed on the borders between their respective territories in December 1920, the Central Committee of the Syrian Union Party (the united Arab nationalist movement at that time) unanimously decided to 'protest against this by all means, based on the legitimate rights of our nation'. It added that it rejected any border separating Palestine from the rest of Syria, protested against any partition of the country, and demanded, after denouncing the occupation, complete independence.[8]

To further affirm the struggle for unity, a national congress was held in Geneva, attended by nationalists from across Syria and Palestine, which eventually led to the formation of 'The Syrian–Palestinian Congress'. In a memorandum submitted to the Genoa Economic and Financial Conference, held on the 12th of May 1925, it was noted that the division of Syria into small states aimed to foster local rivalries, based on the principle of 'divide and rule', and that 'the existence of independent states within a small country, especially at the level of economy and security, threatens overall stability and undermines commerce and economic life'.[9]

This struggle was not limited to the Syrian-Palestinian Congress operating abroad. A domestic nationalist movement, represented in early 1925 by a delegation from Damascus, met with the French High Commissioner and declared: 'We demand that the Syrian lands, with their natural borders before World War I, including the Alawite regions, Jabal al-Druze, the Sanjak of Alexandretta, and the lands annexed to the Mount Lebanon Mutasarrifate, be recognised as one nation in language and nationalism'.

Sectarian regionalism began to emerge, but at the same time, it faced economic difficulties that revived nationalist sentiments. For example, both issues were addressed in a memorandum sent by the leaders of Jabal al-Druze to the

8 Said n.d., vol. 3, p. 263.

9 Said n.d., p. 275.

French High Commissioner in June 1925: 'Jabal al-Druze is an integral part of Syria, sharing its language and ethnicity, and connected to it through comprehensive economic relationships. Damascus takes its supplies from Al-Jabal, while Al-Jabal imports all its necessary goods from Damascus. They have a long-standing and strong bond'.

It was also stated that Jabal al-Druze wished to maintain its form of government and administrative autonomy in all fields. However, the features of this regional-sectarian approach diminished during the revolutionary rise of the nationalist struggle against French imperialism. When the revolution of 1925 erupted, it began in Jabal al-Druze, under the military leadership of Sultan al-Atrash.[10] Its approach was nationalist, transcending both regionalism and sectarianism. This was most clearly expressed in Sultan al-Atrash's first declaration after being appointed as a general leader by the nationalist movement:

> O sons of glorious Arabs ... O Arab Syrians, remember your ancestors, history, martyrs, and national honor. The colonisers have stolen our property and seized the resources of our lands, erecting harmful barriers within the same nation. They have divided us into nations, sects, and states, and deprived us of our freedom of religion, thought, conscience, and even the ability to travel within our own lands and provinces (23 August 1925).

The revolution continued under the banner of recognising a unified, independent Arab Syrian state and called for the unification of all Syrian regions – both coastal and inland – and the establishment of a popular government that would convene a constituent assembly to draft a basic law based on the principle of absolute national sovereignty. Throughout this turbulent period, the nationalist movement repeatedly called for caution against sectarian hostilities and emphasised the importance of Arab unity. This was supported by widespread popular participation in the revolution, which extended to other regions of the state and erupted in both urban and rural areas.

During the revolution, the French played a despicable role in fostering sectarian division and dispersion to suppress the uprising. To achieve this, they recruited a Muslim group from Lebanon to attack Christians in Hasbaya and

10 Sultan al-Atrash (1891–1982) was a prominent Druze leader and Syrian nationalist who led the Great Syrian Revolt (1925–7) against French Mandate rule. Born into an influential Druze family in Jabal al-Druze, he organised armed resistance that spread from the Druze Mountain to Damascus and other parts of Syria. After the revolt's suppression, he lived in exile before returning to Syria upon independence. He remained an important symbol of Syrian resistance and Arab nationalism until his death. (A.K.)

Rashaya. However, the revolution's leaders exposed these imperialist motives, reaffirmed their nonsectarian nationalist goals, and avoided direct confrontation with this group. In one instance, they besieged the conspirators, disarmed them, and sent them back to Jdeideh, demonstrating the revolution's true intentions. Although the revolution failed to expel the French imperialists, it deeply undermined imperialism and established revolutionary traditions that ultimately helped prevent the fragmentation of Syria into small sectarian states.

3 An Attempt to Transform the Religious Sects into Nationalities

To deepen sectarianism, imperialists attempted to convince certain religious sects that they were 'independent nationalities'. This was the goal of the French in fragmenting Syria into small sectarian states. Similarly, the British aimed to achieve the same in Egypt by spreading the claim that the Copts, the largest Christian bloc, constituted a nation distinct from the rest of the Egyptians. The British argued that the Copts were part of the original Egyptian population, while Muslims descended from Arabs who migrated to Egypt and seized the land in the seventh century CE. However, British imperialism failed to convince the Copts of this divisive claim. The Copts, in fact, played a significant role in the nationalist movement, with many participating in the leadership of political parties, particularly the Wafd Party, which led the national struggle.

Nevertheless, Britain persisted in claiming that one of the reasons for its opposition to Egyptian independence and withdrawal was its desire to protect the interests of minorities, particularly the Copts and foreign communities. This claim garnered support among imperialist collaborators, yet it ultimately failed to secure Britain's position. The nationalist movement compelled Britain to withdraw politically, militarily, and economically from Egypt. Following the British withdrawal, sectarian tensions and confrontations diminished, as reactionaries from both religious sects lost their imperialist backing, and national developments helped to reduce attempts at incitement.

Now that Arab nationalist movements had won the battle, vanquishing French and British imperialism and achieving political and economic independence to varying degrees, sectarian disputes were rapidly settled. An exception to this was Lebanon, where major state positions and parliamentary seats continued to be distributed on a sectarian basis. As a result, it was natural that the call to abolish sectarian distribution was a key demand of the democratic progressive movement in Lebanon.

4 The Israeli Attempt

The Israeli ruling elites followed the path of the imperialists by refusing to recognise the Arabs in Israel as a national minority, instead classifying them as sectarian minorities. The official discourse continues to insist on this approach, referring to them as 'minority groups'. Additionally, Israel made efforts to separate the Druze from the Arab minority, treating them as a distinct nationality. To this end, the state favoured the Druze over Muslims, established religious courts exclusively for them, and promoted the claim that they were equal to Jewish citizens.

In this context, the Israeli state found its only support among reactionary elements, as adherents of other religious sects rejected this fragmentation and affirmed their unified Arab national identity. Druze adherents followed a similar path, and they continue to lead a struggle against certain reactionary leaders who collaborated with Israeli ruling circles. Their aim is to exclude these leaders from positions of authority and strengthen their Arab national identity. Sectarianism, therefore, has emerged as a reactionary and imperialist tool, and its complete defeat will only be achieved by eradicating both reactionism and imperialism through a united national struggle.

Bibliography

Al-Afghani, Said 1960, *Aswaq al-Arab fi al-Jahiliyya wa al-Islam* [Arab Markets in Pre-Islamic and Islamic Times], 2nd ed., Damascus: Dar al-Fikr.

Al-Alusi, Shihab al-Din Mahmud 1867–71, *Bulugh al-Arab fi Marifat Ahwal al-Arab* [The Attainment of Knowledge of the Conditions of the Arabs], 4 volumes, Cairo: al-Matbaa al-Amira.

Al-Amin, Sayyid Muhsin 1983, *Aʿyan al-Shiʿa*, vol. 1., Beirut: Dar al-Taʿaruf.

Al-Azm, Sadiq Jalal 1968, *Naqd al-Fikr al-Dini* [Critique of Religious Thought], Beirut: Dar al-Talia.

Al-Azm, Sadiq Jalal 1970, *al-Naqd al-Dhati bad al-Hazima* [Self-Criticism after the Defeat], Beirut: Dar al-Talia.

Al-Husari, Sati 1963, *Ma Hiya al-Qawmiya: Abhath wa Dirasat ala Dhaw al-Ahdath wa al-Nadhariyat* [What is nationalism? enquiries and studies in light of events and theories], Beirut: Dar al-Ilm lil-Malayin.

Al-Husari, Sati 1965, *Al-Bilad al-Arabiyyah wa al-Dawlah al-Uthmaniyyah* [The Arab Countries and the Ottoman State], 3rd edition, Beirut: Dar al-Ilm lil-Malayin.

Ali, Syed Amir 1938 [1924], *Mukhtasar Tarikh al-Arab wa al-Tamaddun al-Islami* [A Brief History of the Arabs and Islamic Civilization], Cairo: Matbaat Lajnat al-Talif wa al-Tarjama wa al-Nashr.

Al-Ittihad 1985, 'A glimpse into the life of our late comrade, Emile Tuma', 28 August [In Arabic].

Al-Ittihad 2019, 'An enlightening struggle biography: Emile Tuma 1919–1985', 15 November [In Arabic].

Al-Jawzi, Bandali 1928, *min Tarikh al-Harakat al-Fikriyya fi al-Islam* [History of Islamic Intellectual Movements], Jerusalem: Bayt al-Maqdis Press.

Al-Jawzi, Bandali 2015, *Tarikh al-Harakat al-Fikriyya fi al-Islam* [History of Intellectual Movements in Islam], Jerusalem: Bayt al-Maqdis.

Al-Kawakibi, Abd al-Rahman 1902, *Tabayi al-Istibdad wa-Masari al-Istibad* [The Nature of Tyranny and the Struggles of Enslavement], Cairo: Matbaat al-Hilal.

Al-Khatib, Anwar 1959, *al-Nazah al-Ishtirakiyya fi al-Islam* [The Socialist Tendency in Islam], Cairo: Maktabat al-Nahda al-Misriyya.

Al-Khudari, Muhammad n.d., *Muhadarat fi Tarikh al-Umam al-Islamiyya* [Lectures on the History of Islamic Nations], 10th ed., Cairo: The Cairo Commercial.

Al-Qasi, Allal 1947, *Tarikh al-Harakat al-Istiqlaliyya fi al-Maghrib al-Arabi* [History of Independence Movements in the Arab Maghreb], Cairo: Al-Risala Print House.

Al-Raziq, Ali Abd 1925, *al-Islam w-Usul al-Hokm* [Islam and the Foundations of Governance], Cairo: Dar al-Hilal.

Al-Ṣadr, Muḥammad Bāqir 1984, *Fadalat al-Imam*, Beirut: Dar al-Taʿaruf.

Al-Sharif, M. 1991, 'Study: Emile Tuma and his role in utilizing history in the struggle for Palestinian national culture', *Al-Ittihad*, 5 December, p. 8 [In Arabic].

Al-Shmali, Abdo n.d., *Tarikh al-falsafa al-Arabiyya al-Islamiyya wa Athar Rijalha* [History of Arab-Islamic Philosophy and the Influence of Its Men].

Al-Tabari, Muhammad ibn Jarir 1987, *The History of al-Tabari* (*Tarikh al-rusul wal-muluk*), vol. 32, *The Reunification of the Abbasid Caliphate*, translated and annotated by C.E. Bosworth, Albany: State University of New York Press.

Al-Thalabi n.d., *Muhadarat al-udaba*, vol. 1.

Ali, Sayyid Amir n.d. *Mukhtasar Tarikh al-'Arab wa-l-Tamaddun al-Islami* [A Short History of the Arabs and Islamic Civilization], Cairo.

Allush, Naji 1960, *al-Thawri al-'Arabi al-Mu'asir* [The Contemporary Arab Revolutionary], Beirut: Dar al-Talia.

Althusser, Louis 1971, *Lenin and Philosophy and Other Essays*, translated by Ben Brewster, London: New Left Books.

Amal, Iskandar. 1989, *Studies on the works of Dr. Emile Tuma*, Haifa [In Arabic].

Amin, Ahmad 1933, *Duha al-Islam* [The Early Days of Islam], vol. 1, 7th ed., Cairo: Maktabat al-Nahda al-Misriyya.

Amin, Ahmad 1964, *Fajr al-Islam* [Early Islam], 9th ed., Cairo: Maktabat al-Nahda al-Misriyya.

Amin, Ahmad n.d., *Duha al-Islam* [The Early Days of Islam], vol. 3, 7th ed., Cairo: Maktabat al-Nahda al-Misriyya.

Baron, Salo Wittmayer 1947, *Modern Nationalism and Religion*, New York: Harper & Brothers Publishers.

Beinin, Joel 1990, *Was the Red Flag Flying There? Marxist Politics and the Arab-Israeli Conflict in Egypt and Israel, 1948–1965*, Berkeley: University of California Press.

Budeiri, Musa 1979, *The Palestine Communist Party 1919–1948: Arab and Jew in the Struggle for Internationalism*, London: Ithaca Press.

Crone, Patricia 2004, *God's Rule: Government and Islam*, New York: Columbia University Press.

Darawzah, Muhammad Izzat 1957, *Al-Wihdah Al-'Arabiyyah* [Arab Unity], Cairo: Al-Maktab At-Tijari Lit-Tiba'ah wat-Tawzi' wan-Nashr.

Engels, Friedrich 1877, 'Introduction', *Anti-Dühring*, available at: https://www.marxists.org/archive/marx/works/1877/anti-duhring/introduction.htm.

Engels, Friedrich 1880, 'Introduction', *Socialism: Utopian and Scientific*, available at: https://www.marxists.org/archive/marx/works/1880/soc-utop/int-mat.htm.

Engels, Friedrich 1883, 'Karl Marx's Funeral', *Der Sozialdemokrat*, 22 March, available at: https://www.marxists.org/archive/marx/works/1883/death/dersoz1.htm.

Engels, Friedrich 1894–95, 'On the History of Early Christianity', *Die Neue Zeit*, available at: https://www.marxists.org/archive/marx/works/1894/early-christianity/.

Farah, Pulus 1962, *Muqaddimat fi Tarikh al-'Arab al-Ijtima'i* [Introduction to the Social History of the Arabs], Beirut: al-Kitab al-'Arabi.

Ghannan, Muhammad Abdullah 1959, *Al-Hakim bi-Amr Allah wa-Asrar al-Dawa al-Fatimiyya* [Al-Hakim bi-Amr Allah and the Secrets of the Fatimid Mission], 2nd edition, Cairo.

Gramsci, Antonio 1971, *Selections from the Prison Notebooks*, edited by Quintin Hoare and Geoffrey Nowell Smith, New York: International Publishers.

Grunebaum, Gustav Edmund von 1956, *Hadarat al-Islam* [Medieval Islam], translated by Abd al-Aziz Tawfiq Jawid, Cairo: Maktabat Misr.

Hanafi, Hassan 1991, *al-Turath wa al-Tajdid* [Heritage and Renewal], Cairo: al-Markaz al-ʿArabi li al-Bahth wa al-Nashr.

Hitti, Philip K. 1952, *History of the Arabs*, vol. 2, Beirut: Dar al-Kashshaf.

Hitti, Philip K. 1970, *History of the Arabs: From the Earliest Times to the Present*, 10th ed., London: Macmillan.

Ibn Khaldun, Abd al-Rahman n.d., *al-Muqaddima*, Beirut: Dar al-Kitab al-Lubnani.

Jordaq, Jorj n.d., *Imam Ali Sawt al-Adala al-Insaniyya* [Imam Ali: The Voice of Human Justice], Beirut: Dar al-Kotob al-Ilmiyah.

Kassab, Elizabeth Suzanne 2010, *Contemporary Arab Thought: Cultural Critique in Comparative Perspective*, New York: Columbia University Press.

Khusraw, Nasir-i 1970, *Safar-nama*, translated by Yahya al-Khashshab, Beirut: Dar al-Kitab al-Jadid.

Lenin, Vladimir Ilyich 1913, 'The National Question in Our Programme', 7 May, available at: https://www.marxists.org/archive/lenin/works/1913/may/07b.htm.

Lenin, Vladimir Ilyich 1914, *The Right of Nations to Self-Determination*, available at: https://www.marxists.org/archive/lenin/works/1914/self-det/.

Lutsky, V. 1971, *Tarikh al-Aqtar al-Arabiyya al-Hadith* [Modern History of Arab Countries], Moscow: Dar al-Taqadum.

Macdonald, D.B. 1903, *Development of Muslim Theology, Jurisprudence, and Constitutional Theory*, New York: Charles Scribner's Sons.

Marx, Karl 1859, 'Preface to A Contribution to the Critique of Political Economy', available at: https://www.marxists.org/archive/marx/works/1859/critique-pol-economy/preface.htm.

Muruwwa, Hussein 1978–9, *al-Nazʿat al-Madiyya fi al-Falsafa al-ʿArabiyya al-Islamiyya* [Materialist Tendencies in Arab-Islamic Philosophy], 2 volumes, Beirut: Dar al-Farabi.

Muruwwa, Hussein 1988, *al-Nazʿat al-Madiyya fi al-Falsafa al-ʿArabiyya al-Islamiyya* [Materialist Tendencies in Arab-Islamic Philosophy], Beirut: Dar al-Farabi.

Pappe, Ilan 2006, *The Ethnic Cleansing of Palestine*, Oxford: Oneworld.

Pappe, Ilan 2011, *The Rise and Fall of a Palestinian Dynasty: The Husaynis, 1700–1948*, Berkeley: University of California Press.

Rida, Muhammad Rashid 1921, *Tarikh al-Imam Muhammad ʿAbdu* [The History of Imam Muhammad Abduh], Cairo: Dar al-Manar.

Rida, Muhammad Rashid 1922, *al-Khilafa aw al-Imama al-ʿUzma* [The Caliphate or the Great Imamate], Cairo: al-Manar Press.

Robinson, James Harvey 1926, *Medieval and Modern Times*, Boston: Ginn and Company.

Rodinson, Maxime 1973 [1966], *Islam and Capitalism*, translated by Brian Pearce, London: Allen Lane.

Rodinson, Maxime 1981, *Islam and Capitalism*, London: Penguin Books.

Said, Amin 1930, *al-Arab wa-al-Turk fi Ahd al-Dustur* [Arabs and Turks in the Constitutional Era], Beirut: al-Maktabah al-Arabiyyah.

Said, Amin n.d., *Thawrat al-ʿArab, Muqaddimatuha – Asbabuha – Nataijuha* [The Arab Revolt: Its Preliminaries – Its Causes – Its Results], Cairo: Al-Muqattam Print House.

Salih, Ahmad Abbas 1972, *al-Yamin wal-Yasar fi al-Islam* [The Right and the Left in Islam], Beirut: al-Muassasa al-ʿArabiyya lil-Dirasat wa-l-Nashr.

Salih, Ahmad Abbas 1973, *al-Yamin wal-Yasar fi al-Islam* [The Right and the Left in Islam], Beirut: al-Muassasa al-ʿArabiyya lil-Dirasat wa-l-Nashr.

Sayigh, Yezid 1997, *Armed Struggle and the Search for State: The Palestinian National Movement, 1949–1993*, Oxford: Oxford University Press.

Shawqi, Muhammad 1954, *Al-Ikhwan al-Muslimun wal-Mujtamaʿ al-Misri* [The Muslim Brotherhood and Egyptian Society], Cairo: Maktabat Wahba.

Sonn, Tamara 1996, *Interpreting Islam: Bandali Jawzi's Islamic Intellectual History*, New York: Oxford University Press.

Tarabishi, Jurj 1982, *min al-Nahda ila al-Ridda* [From Renaissance to Apostasy], London: Riad el-Rayyes.

Tarabishi, Jurj 1993, *Madhbahat al-Turath fi al-Thaqafa al-ʿArabiyya al-Muʿasira* [The Massacre of Heritage in Contemporary Arab Culture], London: Riad el-Rayyes.

Tawfiq, Hussein Muhammad 1953, *Hadha al-Alam al-Arabi* [This Arab World], Beirut: Dar al-Ilm lil-Malayin.

Tizzini, T. 1978, *Project for a New Vision of Arab Thought in the Middle Ages*, Damascus: Dar Dimashq [In Arabic].

Tuma, Emile. 1979a, *Social movements in Islam*, Jerusalem: Manshurat Salah al-Din [In Arabic].

Tuma, Emile. 1979b, *The Modern History of Arab Peoples' Journey*, Beirut: Dar al-Farabi. [In Arabic].

Tuma, Emile. 1978, 'The Position on Cultural Heritage', *al-Jadid*, 24, 8: 5–9. [In Arabic].

Wolfenson, Israel 1927, *Tarikh al-Yahud fi Bilad al-ʿArab* [The History of the Jews of Arabia], Cairo: Maktabat al-Thaqafa al-Diniyya.

Yale, William 1958, *The Near East: A Modern History*, Ann Arbor: University of Michigan Press.

Zaydan, Jurji 1922, *Tarikh al-Tamaddun al-Islami* [History of Islamic Civilization], vol. 4, 3rd ed., Cairo: Matbaat al-Hilal.

Index of Modern Authors

General Index (Names and Subjects)

www.ingramcontent.com/pod-product-compliance
Lightning Source LLC
LaVergne TN
LVHW020045251026
850939LV00004B/39